# Paradox® 4

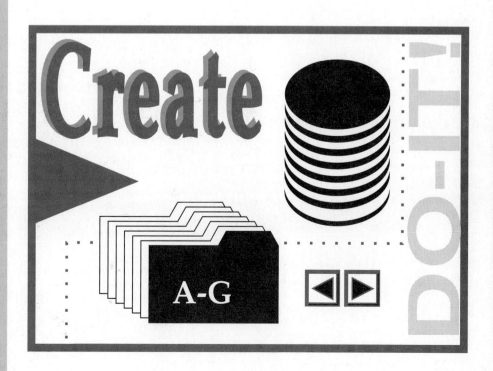

# Paradox® 4: A Short Course

## Michael A. Henry

**COMPASS Series**

Dennis P. Curtin, *Series Editor*

**REGENTS/PRENTICE HALL**
Englewood Cliffs, New Jersey 07632

**Library of Congress Cataloging-in-Publication Data**
Henry, Michael A.
    Paradox 4 : a short course / Michael A. Henry.
        p.   cm. — (Computer application software series)
    Includes index.
    ISBN 0-13-035668-9
    1. Data base management.  2. Paradox (Computer file)  I. Title.
    II. Series: Computer application software series.
QA76.76.D3H4764  1993
005.75'65—dc20                                    93-18667
                                                    CIP

Acquisitions editor: Liz Kendall
Editorial/production supervision: Cecil Yarbrough
Copy editor: Elyse Duffy
Designer and half-title illustrator: Janis Owens
Cover designer: Marianne Frasco
Desktop publishing: Cathleen Morin
Manufacturing buyer: Ed O'Dougherty
Supplements editor: Cindy Harford
Editorial assistant: Jane Avery

Cover art: Compass dial printed from a copper plate
made by Samuel Emery of Salem, Massachusetts (1809-1882),
by permission of the Peabody Museum of Salem

© 1993 by REGENTS/PRENTICE HALL
A Division of Simon & Schuster
Englewood Cliffs, New Jersey 07632

Printed in the United States of America
10  9  8  7  6  5  4  3  2  1

ISBN 0-13-035668-9

Prentice-Hall International (UK) Limited, *London*
Prentice-Hall of Australia Pty. Limited, *Sydney*
Prentice-Hall of Canada Inc., *Toronto*
Prentice-Hall Hispanoamericana, S.A., *Mexico*
Prentice-Hall of India Private Limited, *New Delhi*
Prentice-Hall of Japan, Inc., *Tokyo*
Simon & Schuster Asia Ptd. Ltd., *Singapore*
Editora Prentice-Hall do Brasil, Ltda., *Rio de Janeiro*

*As always, for Carla.*

*This time, thank you for your patience.*

# CONTENTS

# CONTENTS

This text will introduce you to Paradox 4, a popular database management program. To make your introduction as simple as possible, the text is organized into topics and chapters.

### Topics: The Basic Unit

The basic unit of this text is the topic, a short section that focuses on a specific procedure or task. This makes it easier for you to study specific operations as compared to a book with traditional chapter organization. Short topics are less intimidating than long chapters, and they make it easier for your instructor to assign specific sections.

Each topic contains the following elements:

- *Objectives* explain what you will be able to accomplish when you finish the topic.
- *Introductory concepts* introduce the basic principles in the topic. These principles will apply throughout Paradox 4, but many also apply to other microcomputer programs. When you understand the concepts, procedures are easier to learn because everything fits into a framework. Being able to use concepts makes it easier to transfer your knowledge to other programs and other computers.
- *Tutorials* demonstrate step by step how to use the procedures discussed in the topic. If you follow the instructions, you will quickly see how each procedure is performed and be able to observe the results immediately. The procedures are discussed in detail in the following section.
- The *Quick Reference* section describes the execution of each command step by step. This section serves a dual function: you can refer to it while using the text, or you can use it later when you are working on projects of your own.
- *Exercises* provide an opportunity for you to practice and gain experience with the concepts and procedures discussed in the topic. Unlike the tutorials, the exercises do not guide you step by step. They are similar to the tutorials, but you will have to determine which procedures need to be used.

### Chapters: A Pause for Reinforcement

Related topics are grouped into chapters so you can pause to review and test yourself. At the end of each chapter are the following sections you should complete:

- A review of the key concepts that were discussed in the chapter.
- A series of questions that measure your ability to use the concepts and procedures discussed in the chapters. There are three types of questions: Fill In the Blank, Match the Columns, and Write Out the Answers.

**Do You Need Incentive?**

Workers who use computers, but who are similar in every other respect to workers who do not use them, earn a fat bonus of 10 to 15 percent for their knack with these machines.

The New York Times, *February 14, 1992, page D2, referring to a study by Alan B. Krueger of Princeton University.*

**JUMP-START TUTORIAL**

The computer is an enticing, interactive tool, not a passive device you just read about. To encourage this hands-on flavor, this text begins with a jump-start tutorial that lets you work with the computer and Paradox immediately. This tutorial not only lets you begin sooner but also gives you an overview of what the program can do.

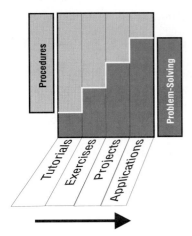
- Projects that build skills and introduce some problems to be solved. You will find background material for each project, but no specific procedures are given. In order to complete the projects, you must already have mastered the topics in the chapter or go back into the text and look up the information you need.

### Hands-On Lab Activities

In a lab-oriented course, your progress and enjoyment depend on the quality of the hands-on activities used to teach the concepts and procedures. Ideally, these activities perform a number of useful functions:

- They build skills in the specific procedures that you will need to use.
- They provide motivation.
- They illustrate a variety of situations in which the specific procedures are used.
- They introduce important principles that you will encounter in business and in other courses in the curriculum.
- They help you to develop problem-solving skills. Exercises provide less guidance than the tutorials, and the projects and applications provide even less. Moving through this sequence of activities challenges you to think about what you should do and why you need to do it.

This text includes dozens of such activities and presents them on four levels: tutorials, exercises, projects, and applications. To complete each level you must have an increasingly better understanding of Paradox 4.

- Tutorials introduce a specific procedure or a group of closely related procedures. Their purpose is to demonstrate how the procedures work and to show the effects they have.
- Exercises at the end of each topic reinforce the concepts and procedures that have been discussed. You will have to rely on your experience with the tutorial and refer to the Quick Reference section to find the information you need to complete them. This refines your ability to look up information needed to complete tasks—something that you will need to do on your own when the class is over.
- Projects at the end of each chapter are similar to the exercises, but to complete them you need to use the information in more than one topic.
- Real-World Applications in Chapter 8 require a firm ability to apply the procedures discussed in the text. Unlike projects, these applications test your accumulated skills after the text is completed. These projects are organized into three separate tracks: a job-search kit, a research paper, and a business plan. Your instructor may assign different applications to different classes or to different groups within the class.

### Key Features

This text has a number of features that distinguish it from other texts in this area.

- A *jump-start tutorial* is in Topic 1 so you can begin working on the computer from the very first day. This tutorial is designed to give

**Student Resource Disks**
Many of the files on which you work are on the *Student Resource Disk* which your instructor will make available to you.

you an idea of how the Paradox 4 program works and to demonstrate some of the things it can do.

- This text goes beyond procedures. Its activities are not boring "make-work activities." In many cases the activities introduce you to other subject areas and encourage you to think about *problem solving*—not just pushing buttons.

- To reduce the amount of typing or data-entry time, many exercises are based on files that are provided on the *Student Resource Disk.* This disk is available from your instructor.

- The database files used in tutorials, exercises, projects, and applications are designed to be *real-world* in nature and represent some of the activities that you will encounter in business and other courses in the curriculum.

- In the process of completing this text, you will work with more than ten database files (not including those derived from this core group or those created "from scratch").
  - OVERVIEW is an inventory database used in the Jump-Start Tutorial in Topic 1. It introduces databases and Paradox 4. It is then reused occasionally in other chapters in the text.
  - CUSTOMER and PURCHASE are database files for a toy store called Alice's Wonderland; they contain customer and accounting data. These files are used in the tutorials in every topic.
  - EMPLOYEE and TIME are corporate database files that store employee records and the hours employees have worked. These files are used in the exercises at the end of every topic.
  - TITLES and SALES are two files from a publishing company that track titles and sales in various markets. These files are used in the projects at the end of each chapter.
  - JOBSRCH, TERMPAPR, and INVENTRY are database files used to store job-search contacts, references for a term paper, and a business inventory tracking system. These files are used in the real-world applications at the end of the text.

- You will find that you first use this text to structure your learning, and then later as a reference. By referring to the list of topics on the back cover, you can locate a topic of interest quickly, then skim the Quick Reference section in that topic to find the information you need.

- There is an appendix about DOS at the end of the text. If you are unfamiliar with system software, you can follow the step-by-step instructions in this appendix to format disks, copy (and delete) files, specify paths, and manage directories.

- At the back of the book are a cardboard punch-out *keyboard template* and *pocket guide* for Paradox 4.

### Getting Ready

Before you proceed with the activities in this text, consider these points:

- Save all of your files on a floppy disk and make regular backup copies of this disk.

- Occasionally you will find notations such as VIEW <filename>. Substitute your own filenames for the brackets and the text within them. For example, if you want to work with a file named MYFILE and you see the instruction VIEW <filename>, type (or select) VIEW MYFILE.

## REAL-WORLD APPLICATIONS

The final chapter in this text introduces you to three applications of Paradox that are typical of those you might encounter in the real world outside the classroom. To complete these applications you must solve specific problems on your own.

**Application 1: A Job-Search Kit**
In this application you create a database in which to store information about job interviews you are scheduling or have already had..

**Application 2: A Research Paper**
This application creates a Paradox file in which to store information about works cited in a college research paper.

**Application 3: A Business Plan**
In this application you create a database in which to store company inventory records.

## Supplements

The publisher has developed many supplements for this text that are free to instructors on adoption.

■ *Instructor's Manual with Tests and Resource Disks* by Donna M. Matherly contains suggested course outlines for a variety of course lengths and formats, chapter summaries, teaching tips for each topic, competencies to be attained, solutions and answers to in-text activities, competency production tests, a test bank of 300 objective questions, and a number of supplementary problems.

    Two types of disks are included with this supplement:

  ● *Student Resource Disk* contains the unformatted files to be used to complete the hands-on activities in this text. This master disk can be duplicated for students. Arrangements can be made to have the *Student Resource Disk* bound to copies of this text for an additional fee—contact your Regents/Prentice Hall representative to make arrangements.

  ● *Instructor's Resource Disk* contains files for chapter summaries, competencies, topic goals and tips, solutions for hands-on activities, competency tests, and supplementary problems.

■ *Course Outlines on Disk* contains files and other information from the Instructor's Manual which allow the professor to customize lecture outlines and course syllabi with ease.

■ *Test Manager* is a test generating package that allows professors to customize the test questions contained in the Instructor's Manual. Users can edit, add to, and scramble test questions.

■ A video covering Paradox (Video Professor) is available to qualified adopters.

## Acknowledgments

At this point I would like to thank some of the other people involved in the production of this book. First, I would like to thank Dennis Curtin and Liz Kendall for allowing me to participate in this series and Cecil Yarbrough, who coordinated this book's production. Next, Elyse Duffy for her valuable input during copy editing and keystroke testing. Cathy Morin electronically prepared the layout and format of the text. Jane Avery helped keep the project going from behind the scenes. I would also like to thank Karen Johnson and Carolyn Scott for "keeping me educated."

This text uses the following conventions for commands and prompts.

**Commands**

- Keys you press in sequence are separated by commas. For example, if you are to press F8, release it, and then press Enter←, the instructions read F8, Enter←.
- Keys you press simultaneously are separated by dashes. For example, if you are to hold down Ctrl while you press F8, the instructions read Ctrl-F8.

**Prompts**

All prompts, messages, and field names are shown *in this typeface*. When a prompt appears, you have two choices: Either press a key to make a selection from a menu or type a response and then press Enter←. All keys you press (except those in boxes such as Enter←) and all characters you type are shown in the typeface used here for **FILENAME**.

Filenames are presented in all capital letters, while window names are capitalized: the OVERVIEW file; the Query window. Menu names are shown in capital letters, while options from menus are capitalized: Open the TOOLS menu, choose Info, then Structure, and press Enter←.

# Paradox® 4

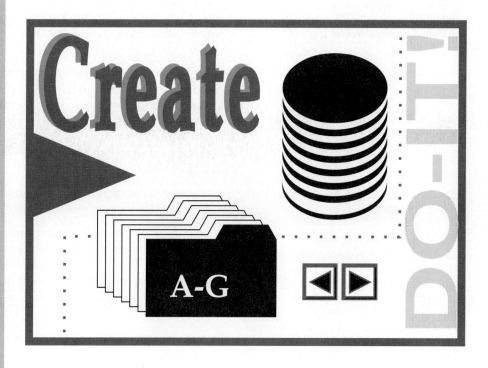

# Getting Started

## Paradox 4—An Overview

> **After completing this topic, you will be able to:**
> - Describe the differences between record management and database management programs
> - Explain the concept of a relational database
> - Load Paradox on your computer system
> - Open an existing database file
> - Print data that are displayed in a window
> - Exit the Paradox program

One of the most important applications available for microcomputers is the management of databases. A *database* is one or more files that contain an organized collection of information. For example, when you make a reservation with an airline, your name and address are entered into a database. At the same time, a seat on a specific flight is reserved for you in the same database. Later, if you call the airline with a question or problem, the operator can find out what seat was assigned simply by searching the database.

To create, maintain, and use a database you use a *database management program* such as Paradox. In other words, you can use Paradox to store information, retrieve it anytime you need it, and update it whenever necessary. For example, you can:

- Add new information
- Change or update existing information
- Find specific information
- Arrange the information in a specific order
- Delete information that is no longer needed
- Print reports that contain part or all of the information
- Create new files that contain all or part of the information found in one or more other files

Because it is very flexible and powerful, Paradox can be adapted to perform an almost endless variety of different jobs.

- You can create and maintain mailing lists for sales and marketing purposes, using the data to automatically print letters, envelopes, and mailing labels. You can also use the information to answer questions such as "What phone numbers are listed for SMITH?" or "How many people are listed in zip code 63301?"

**Record Management Programs**
Record management programs can only work with one file at a time. To access the data in another file, you must first remove the first file from memory, then retrieve the new one.

■ You can control the inventory for your company by recording the products and supplies that move into or out of stock. In this case, Paradox can provide answers to questions like "How many SKY HOOKS are left in stock?" or "When was the last shipment of LASERS received?"

■ You can monitor assets such as stock portfolios and always know what stocks you own and how much they are worth. You can ask Paradox, "How many shares of BORLAND stock do I own?", "What stocks have increased in value since the first of the year?" and "What stocks have I bought this month?"

The terms *database* and *database management program* are often used interchangeably. Actually, there are two types of programs used to manage files that contain highly structured data: *record* management programs and *database* management programs. In addition, not all highly structured data files are databases.

### Record Management Programs

Record management programs (sometimes called *flat-file database* programs or *file management programs*) are like those that are built into word processing programs (such as WordPerfect®) or spreadsheet programs (such as Lotus® 1-2-3®). These programs store and maintain data in a single file. When you use a record management program to store data for different aspects of a business, you must use a series of separate fields known as *record files*. If you need to change an entry that is common to two different files, you must load the first file, make the change, then load the second file and make the change there, also. For example, suppose you have one file that contains employees' names, addresses, and telephone numbers and another file that contains payroll information. If one of your employees moves, you will need to update their address in both files. In other words, when you use a record management program, you may need to update more than one file when only one change needs to be made.

### Database Management Programs

As the amount of information you track increases, it quickly becomes inconvenient to use a collection of separate files that contain related or even duplicate entries. For example, an employee's name might appear in several different files such as payroll information, vacation data, and retirement statistics. There are several disadvantages to this duplication:

■ Data must be entered separately into each file
■ It increases the risk of errors in the information
■ More disk space (and memory) is needed to store your data

A database management program eliminates these problems. When you use a database management program, you only need to enter each piece of information one time because the program can use interrelated data even if they are stored in separate files. For example, if your accounting program stores general ledger information in one file, accounts receivable in another, and accounts payable in a third, your database management program can easily access all of the information in all of the files at the same time.

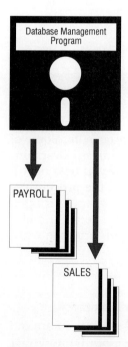

**Database Management Programs**
Database management programs can access the data in more than one file at the same time. This lets you define relationships between the data and reduces the amount of data entry.

## Database Models

When you enter information into a database file, it is organized by the database management program so that it can be located and manipulated easily. The organizational technique used by the program is called the *database model*. Almost all microcomputer database management programs, including Paradox 4, use the *relational model*.

A relational database consists of one or more tables. Each table contains rows and columns much like a spreadsheet. Since a database can contain more than one table, the tables can be *related* to each other. As you will see, you can manipulate the data in related tables to enter, update, and find information stored in the database.

### Relational Database

A relational database file contains columns and rows much like a table. The columns are fields that contain data. The labels at the top of each column are the field names. There are one or more rows of data, and each row is a record.

| ID | LASTNAME | FIRST | STREET | CITY | ST | ZIP | AREA | PHONE |
|----|----------|-------|--------|------|----|----|------|-------|
| 122 | Ranasaurous | Ty | 322 Main Street | St. Louis | MO | 63305 | 314 | 555-1232 |
| 123 | Makit | Willy | 1234 Elm | Los Gatos | CA | 95031 | 415 | 555-2346 |
| 124 | Minut | Ina | 4453 Capitol | Salem | OR | 40000 | 508 | 555-6321 |
| 125 | Schwatrz | Burmuda | 832 Lewis St | Chicago | IL | 20000 | 312 | 555-2311 |
| 115 | Roundalot | Liza | 54321 Second St | Fairlawn | NJ | 30000 | 201 | 555-3433 |
| 113 | Canbe | Titus | 221B Baker St | Salem | OR | 40000 | 508 | 555-3452 |
| 116 | Coopen | Saucer | 3435 Beta Ave | Reading | MA | 20000 | 617 | 555-2342 |
| 120 | Driver | Lori | 654 Alpha St | Atlanta | GA | 30010 | 404 | 555-4572 |
| 119 | Dactal | Terry | 9687 Ballas Dr | Orlando | FL | 32800 | 406 | 555-4357 |
| 117 | Itwork | Will | 422 Olive St | Fairlawn | NJ | 30000 | 201 | 555-2384 |
| 112 | Binone | Ida | 568 Express Dr | Atlanta | GA | 30010 | 404 | 555-0987 |
| 118 | Cross | Chris | 851 Esso Rd | Salem | OR | 40000 | 508 | 555-6345 |
| 114 | Second | Justa | 120 Wentzville | Chicago | IL | 20000 | 312 | 555-6987 |
| 121 | Time | Lotta | 4562 System Dr | St. Louis | MO | 63305 | 314 | 555-3218 |

Field names

Record

Field

---

## JUMP-START TUTORIAL

In this tutorial, you get a jump start on Paradox 4 by following steps that introduce you to the program using an existing database file. Some of the procedures you will be using may seem confusing at first, but remember that the purpose of this tutorial is to show you how useful Paradox can be. You are not expected to retain any of the procedures described here other than those used to load the program and open your files. All of the procedures will be covered in more detail and at a much slower pace later in this text. Relax, have fun, and see what Paradox can do for you.

### WHEN THINGS GO WRONG

If you enter or select a command incorrectly, just press [Esc] and try again. If you are using a mouse, just click anywhere on the screen (except inside an open menu) and the menu will close.

### GETTING STARTED

1. Load the Paradox program into your computer's memory.
   - If you load the program from the operating system command prompt, (for example C> or C:\>), start your computer and refer to "Loading Paradox 4" in the Quick Reference section at the end of this topic.
   - If it is necessary to use another procedure to load the program, such as loading it from a menu or from a network, load the

Paradox program and then start this tutorial at the section "Opening an Existing Database File and Listing Its Records." For future reference, write down the steps that you follow to load the program in the space provided as part of Exercise 1 at the end of this topic.

---

**THE PARADOX OPENING SCREEN**

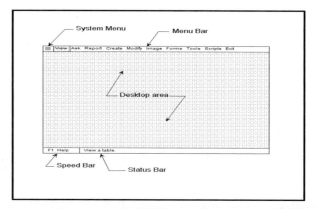

When you load Paradox 4, the copyright screen appears. Press the spacebar and the program's opening screen (also called the *desktop*) appears as shown above.

■ The menu bar at the top of the screen displays a series of options that can be selected in one of three ways.

1. You can use the left and right arrow keys to highlight your choice and then press [Enter ←].

2. You can press the key (usually the first letter) that matches the highlighted letter in your choice.

3. You can position the mouse pointer on your choice and click the left mouse button.

■ The main part of the screen is called the work area. This area will display the windows that contain your data, entry forms, and other items while you work with your database.

■ At the bottom of the screen you will see a status bar or "reminder" line. In the left corner is an area called the speed bar. It reads *F1 Help*. This means you can press [F1] or click on the speed bar at any time to display the on-line help screens. You will also see a short line of text that describes the menu choice that is highlighted on the menu bar.

---

2. Make sure that your printer is ready because you will be sending data to the printer during this tutorial.

## OPENING AN EXISTING DATABASE FILE AND LISTING ITS RECORDS

3. Choose TOOLS from the menu bar. A pull-down menu appears.

4. Insert the original *Student Resource Disk* that accompanies this text into your floppy disk drive.

5. Choose More from the pull-down menu. A second pull-down menu appears. From this menu, choose Directory. When the Directory window appears, select the drive that contains your *Student Resource Disk*.

- If your *Student Resource Disk* is in drive A, type **A:** in the dialog box and press Enter⏎.
- If your *Student Resource Disk* is in drive B: type **B:** in the dialog box and press Enter⏎.

A message appears that says: "Working directory is now A:\ (or B:\)."

6. Choose VIEW from the menu bar. When the dialog box appears, press Enter⏎ or use the mouse to click OK. A list of the data files that are stored on your floppy disk drive is displayed.

7. Use the arrow keys or the mouse to select the file named OVER-VIEW and press Enter⏎ (or click OK). A window opens that lists the data in your file. At the bottom of the window you will see an indicator that says something similar to *1 of 15*. This means that there are 15 records in the database and the current record is number 1. If you use the arrow keys or the mouse pointer and move to a different entry, this indicator changes to reflect your choice.

### PRINTING THE FILE'S RECORDS

8. Open the REPORT menu and choose Output. When the next window appears, press Enter⏎ or click OK. Choose OVERVIEW from the displayed list and press Enter⏎ or click OK. The name of the file (OVERVIEW) displays in the box at the top of the window and a Report Type Selection box opens.

There may be two or more choices in this window, but for now just press Enter⏎ or click OK.

*print* \ 9. When the last selection box appears, choose Printer. The records in the database will print using the Standard Report form.

**Note:** You can also print the records in a file by pressing Alt - F7 anytime a table is displayed.

**Printing Reports**
Here is a typical report as printed from the Paradox REPORT menu. Notice that the name of each field is at the top of each column and a single record appears on each row.

```
2/14/93                  Standard Report                 Page   1


Invoice  Date_ord  Date_out  Product      Model   Price  Qty  Test
-------  --------  --------  -------      -----   -----  ---  ----
1001     1/03/93   1/04/93   Computer     2006    999.50   2   Y
1002     1/03/93   1/05/93   Printer       121    100.50   3   Y
1003     1/03/93   1/03/93   Computer     2006    999.50   1   Y
1004     1/04/93   1/05/93   Modem        1111    175.00   5   N
1005     1/04/93   1/06/93   Monitor       390    500.00   2   N
1006     1/05/93   1/05/93   Network card 1258    375.00   5   N
1007     1/05/93   1/09/93   Modem        1111    175.00   1   N
1008     1/05/93   1/05/93   Tape backup   238    350.00   4   N
1009     1/05/93   1/07/93   Keyboard     3456    125.00   4   N
1010     1/06/93   1/06/93   Hard disk      35    650.00  10   N
1011     1/06/93   1/09/93   CD-ROM        789    500.00   2   N
1012     1/06/93   1/07/93   Printer       121    100.50   5   Y
1013     1/06/93   1/07/93   Monitor       390    500.00   7   N
1014     1/07/93   1/07/93   Computer     1010  1,250.99  10   Y
1015     1/07/93   1/10/93   Printer       121    100.50  20   N
```

### LISTING AND PRINTING THE FILE'S STRUCTURE

10. Open the TOOLS menu and choose Info when the first pull-down menu appears. Choose Structure from the next menu. A selection window opens. Press Enter⏎ or click OK. Finally, select the OVER-VIEW file from the list of files that is displayed and press Enter⏎ or click OK.

A new window opens and displays a list of the fields in the database. The list contains the name of each field and its type and length.

**Viewing the Structure of Your Database**
Open the TOOLS menu, choose Info, then Structure. A display similar to the one shown here appears.

```
2/14/93              Standard Report          Page    1


Field Name                  Field Type
------------------------    ----------
Invoice                     A4
Date_ord                    D
Date_out                    D
Product                     A12
Model                       A4
Price                       $
Qty                         N
Tested                      A1
```

*print*

11. To print the file's structure, open the REPORT menu and select Output. When the Table window appears, press Enter ↵ or click OK. If *STRUCT* is not already highlighted, choose it now and press Enter ↵ or click OK. When the next window opens, press Enter ↵ (or click OK) again.

When the last selection box appears, choose Printer. A list of the fields in the database is printed. When you are finished, use the mouse to click the little box in the upper-left corner of the window (or press Ctrl - F8 ) to close the Structure window.

### BROWSING THROUGH THE FILE'S RECORDS

12. Press End to move the cursor to the end of the database.

The status line at the bottom of the window will now say something similar to *15 of 15* to indicate that the current record is the last one in the database.

13. Press Home to move the cursor to the top of the database.

The status line at the bottom of the window will now say something similar to *1 of 15* to indicate that the current record is the first one in the database.

14. Press the arrow keys to move up or down one line at a time. You can also use PgDn and PgUp to move through the database one screen page at a time.

On the right side of the file list window is a scroll bar. It consists of two arrows (one that points up near the top of the window and one that points down near the bottom) and a small box located in between the arrows. If you click on the up or down arrow with the mouse pointer, your data will move up or down one line at a time. You can also place the mouse pointer on the small box, press and hold the left mouse button and "drag" the data in the window up or down.

If you place the mouse pointer above the small box (but below the up arrow) and click, the data will move up a full screen page. You can also click below the small box and move down one page at a time.

Each row on the screen is a record and each column is a field.

- A record is the database's description of a person, thing, activity, or other item. For example, all of the information on a purchase order could be stored in a single record.

- A field is one part of the description stored in a record. In the current database, the invoice number and the product name are examples of fields.

**NOTE**

If you do not have a window open that displays the data in the OVERVIEW file, repeat Steps 6 and 7. When the data window is redisplayed, continue with the following steps.

**NOTE**

If the data in a window are longer than one screen page, use the scroll bar on the right-hand side of the window. If the data are wider than one screen page, use the scroll bar at the bottom.

## Fields and Records

A database is always organized into fields and records. Fields contain specific information about a person, item, or other subject. A group of fields makes up a record, a complete description of the person, item, or other subject.

| ID | LASTNAME | FIRST | STREET | CITY | ST | ZIP | AREA | PHONE |
|---|---|---|---|---|---|---|---|---|
| 122 | Ranasaurous | Ty | 322 Main Street | St. Louis | MO | 63305 | 314 | 555-1232 |
| 123 | Makit | Willy | 1234 Elm | Los Gatos | CA | 95031 | 415 | 555-2346 |
| 124 | Minut | Ina | 4453 First Capitol | Salem | OR | 40000 | 508 | 555-6321 |
| 125 | Schwatrz | Burmuda | 832 Lewis St | Chicago | IL | 20000 | 312 | 555-2311 |
| 115 | Roundalot | Liza | 54321 Second St | Fairlawn | NJ | 30000 | 201 | 555-3433 |
| 113 | Canbe | Titus | 221B Baker St | Salem | OR | 40000 | 508 | 555-3452 |
| 116 | Coopen | Saucer | 3435 Beta Ave | Reading | MA | 20000 | 617 | 555-2342 |
| 120 | Driver | Lori | 654 Alpha St | Atlanta | GA | 30010 | 404 | 555-4572 |
| 119 | Dactal | Terry | 9687 Ballas Dr | Orlando | FL | 32800 | 406 | 555-4357 |
| 117 | Itwork | Will | 422 Olive St | Fairlawn | NJ | 30000 | 201 | 555-2384 |
| 112 | Binone | Ida | 568 Express Dr | Atlanta | GA | 30010 | 404 | 555-0987 |
| 118 | Cross | Chris | 851 Esso Rd | Salem | OR | 40000 | 508 | 555-6345 |
| 114 | Second | Justa | 120 Wentzville | Chicago | IL | 20000 | 312 | 555-6987 |
| 121 | Time | Lotta | 4562 System Dr | St. Louis | MO | 63305 | 314 | 555-3218 |

**Record**

**Field**

15. If the information in a database is too wide to display at one time, press the right or left arrows keys to view any fields that may be off the screen. When you reach the edge of the data, press the arrow key again and the cursor will "wrap around" to the other side. You can also use your mouse and click the scroll bar at the bottom of the window to help view any fields to the left or right.

## VIEWING SELECTED RECORDS

16. Press F10 and select the ASK menu from the menu bar. When the next window appears, press Enter↵ or click OK to display a list of files. Select the OVERVIEW file and press Enter↵ (or click OK) again. When the Query window appears, use the arrow keys to move the cursor to the first field (just below where it says OVER-VIEW) and press F6. A check mark appears in all of the other fields. Now, use the arrow keys to move to the *Price* field (which may not appear on your screen until you use the arrow keys). Make sure that you are right next to the check mark (not below it) and type **>499**. Finally, press F2.

A new window opens. Only the records with more than *499* in the *Price* field are displayed.

### NOTE

The new window is called an *Answer table*. It is normally sorted by the values in all fields from left to right.

17. Press F10 and select the ASK menu from the menu bar. When the next window appears, press Enter↵ or click OK to display a list of files. Select the OVERVIEW file and press Enter↵ (or click OK) again. Type **<499** in the *Price* field and press F2. Hint: Use ←Bksp to erase the current entry.

A new window opens. Only the records with less than *499* in the *Price* field are displayed.

18. Press F10 and select the ASK menu from the menu bar. When the next window appears, press Enter↵ or click OK to display a list of files. Select the OVERVIEW file and press Enter↵ (or click OK) again. Type **=500** in the *Price* field and press F2. Remember to use ←Bksp to erase the current entry.

A new window opens. Only the records with exactly *500* in the *Price* field are displayed.

19. Press F10 and select the ASK menu from the menu bar. When the next window appears, press Enter↵ or click OK to display a list of files. Select the OVERVIEW file and press Enter↵ (or click OK) again. Use ←Bksp to erase =500 from the *Price* field. Move the cursor to the *Product* field. Make sure that you are right next to the check mark (not below it). Type **Computer** and press F2.

A new window opens. Only the records with *Computer* in the *Product* field are displayed. Notice that when you are searching for text it may be necessary to enter uppercase or lowercase letters exactly as shown in the file.

20. Press F10 and select the ASK menu from the menu bar. When the next window appears, press Enter↵ or click OK to display a list of files. Select the OVERVIEW file and press Enter↵ (or click OK) again. Use ←Bksp to erase *Computer* from the *Product* field. Move the cursor to the *Date_ord* field, type **01/05/93** (right next to the check mark), and press F2.

A new window opens. Only the records with *01/05/93* in the *Date_ord* field are displayed.

## VIEWING SELECTED FIELDS

21. Press F10 and select the ASK menu from the menu bar. When the next window appears, press Enter↵ or click OK to display a list of files. Select the OVERVIEW file and press Enter↵ (or click OK) again. When the Query window appears, use the arrow keys to move the cursor to the first field (Overview) and press F6. The check marks in all of the other fields disappear. Use the arrow keys to move the cursor to the *Price* field, and press F6. A check mark appears. Move to the *Product* field and press F6. Then move to the *Date_ord* field and press F6. Finally, press F2.

A new answer window opens. Only the *Price*, *Product*, and *Date_ord* fields for 01/05/93 are displayed.

## MAKING CALCULATIONS

22. Press F10 and select the ASK menu from the menu bar. When the next window appears, press Enter↵ or click OK to display a list of files. Select the OVERVIEW file and press Enter↵ (or click OK) again. When the Query window appears, remove the check marks from the *Product* and *Date_ord* fields (move to each field and press F6). Move the cursor to the *Price* field. Type **CALC SUM** and press F2.

A new answer window opens. The total of all entries in the *Price* field for 01/05/93 is displayed.

23. Press F10 and select the ASK menu from the menu bar. When the next window appears, press Enter↵ or click OK to display a list of files. Select the OVERVIEW file and press Enter↵ (or click OK) again. If necessary, use the arrow keys to move the cursor to the *Price* field. Edit the *Price* field to read **CALC AVERAGE** and press F2.

A new answer window opens. The average value of all entries in the *Price* field for 01/05/93 is displayed.

**FINISHING UP**

24. Press [Alt]-[F8] (called *Clear All*) to clear the desktop and close any files that may be stored on floppy disks.

25. You have completed this tutorial. You can go on to the next activity or quit for the day. To quit, select EXIT from the menu bar, then select Yes from the pull-down menu. Remove your disks and turn off the computer.

## QUICK REFERENCE

To use Paradox, you must first understand the basic procedures for loading the program, opening and closing files, printing data, and quitting the program.

### ➡ KEY/Strokes

**Loading Paradox 4**

1. Change to the default drive and directory that contains the file PARADOX.EXE.
   - For example, if this file is on drive C, type **C:** and press [Enter ←].
   - If you used the install program that is supplied with Paradox to copy the program to your hard disk, the PARADOX.EXE file will be stored in a directory named PDOX40. To change the directory use the CD command. In other words, to change to the directory named PDOX40, type **CD\PDOX40** and press [Enter ←].
2. Type **PARADOX** and press [Enter ←] to load the program.
   After a short delay, the copyright screen appears.
3. Press the spacebar and the blank Paradox work area (called the desktop) is displayed. At the top of the work area, you will see the Paradox menu bar.

### Changing the Default Disk Drive and Path

When you save or retrieve database files, they are saved to and retrieved from the default drive. You can always tell which drive is currently the default by selecting TOOLS from the menu bar, More from the next menu, and finally, Directory from the last menu. This command sequence displays a small window that shows the current default drive.

To change the default drive, type a new specification in the text box. For example, to change the default drive to A, just type **A:** in the box and press [Enter ←] (or click OK).

### Listing Files on the Disk

To list all files on the default drive, open the TOOLS menu, choose Info, then Inventory. To view only tables, choose Tables from the list. To view other types of files select Files. When the dialog box appears, type a file specification in the box and press [Enter ←] or click OK. You can, if necessary, use DOS wildcards as part of the specification. For example, to view a list of all files on the default drive, type **\*.\*** in the box and press [Enter ←].

### Setting a Path

If your database files are stored in a subdirectory on a disk, you can use the TOOLS-MORE-DIRECTORY command sequence to change the default so that Paradox can locate them. For example, if your files are located in a directory on drive C, named DATABASE, select TOOLS from the menu bar, More from the next menu, and Directory from the last menu. Finally, type **C:\DATABASE** in the text box and press Enter↵ or click OK. ("C:\" may already appear in the text box. If so, just type **DATABASE**.)

When you execute a command to open a file, the program checks the default unless you provide additional instructions. If you need to use a file in a different location, all you need to do is type the disk drive, the path, and the file name in the file selection text box. For example, if you want to view a file that is located in the SAMPLE directory on drive C, start by selecting VIEW from the menu bar. When the dialog box appears, type **C:\SAMPLE** in the box labeled Table, then press Enter↵ or click OK. A list of the available files appears. Select the file that you want to use and press Enter↵ or click OK.

### Opening a Database File

To work with an existing database file, start by selecting VIEW from the menu bar. When the dialog box appears, press Enter↵ or click OK. A list of the available files appears. Select the file that you want to use and press Enter↵ or click OK. Paradox loads the file into memory.

### Printing Data

To print the data in a table, select REPORT from the menu bar. When the pull-down menu opens, choose Output. A dialog box appears. Press Enter↵ or click OK and you will see a list of files. Select the file that you need to print and press Enter↵ or click OK again. Choose the name of the report that you want to use from the list and press Enter↵ or click OK.

### Quitting Paradox

*Ex 9*
*Pg 20*

Before you leave Paradox, you must make sure that all files are closed and your desktop is clear. To do so, press Alt - F8 (to clear the desktop), select EXIT from the menu bar, and choose Yes from the pull-down menu. Paradox closes and the DOS prompt reappears.

▶ **E X E R C I S E S**

---

### EXERCISE 1

---

### LOADING PARADOX 4 ON YOUR SYSTEM

If your Paradox program is on a network or if your system has been customized, you may need to follow a procedure that is different from the one that is discussed in this topic. If that is the case, use this space to list the steps that you need to use to load the program.

1. _____
2. _____
3. _____
4. _____
5. _____

## EXERCISE 2

### COPYING STUDENT RESOURCE DISK FILES

In this exercise, you will copy files from the original *Student Resource Disk* to your working disk. The instructions in this exercise assume that you are working on a computer that is able to display the DOS command prompt. If you are working on a system connected to a network or one that has a customized menu, you may need to follow a different procedure. If this is the case, ask your instructor or system administrator for help.

1. Start your computer (or quit Paradox) so that the DOS command prompt is displayed.
2. Place the *Student Resource Disk* in an appropriate drive. Have a blank, formatted disk ready to copy files onto.
3. If your resource disk is in drive A, type **DISKCOPY A: A:**, (if it is in drive B, type **DISKCOPY B: B:**) and press Enter←. As the copy process continues, you will be prompted periodically to swap disks.
4. When the copy process ends, the system will display a message that reads: *Copy another? (Y/N)*. Type **N** (for No) and press Enter←.
5. When the DOS prompt reappears, remove your disk.
6. Put the original disk in a safe place, label the new disk, and use it for all of your work throughout the remainder of this text.

> Paradox Data Disk (backup)
> Your name
> Date:
> Class:

**The Disk Label**
After copying your Paradox data files to a disk, you should label the new disk so that it doesn't get lost or inadvertently erased.

## EXERCISE 3

### IDENTIFYING THE ITEMS ON THE SCREEN

1. Identify the parts of the Paradox screen that are shown in the following illustration.

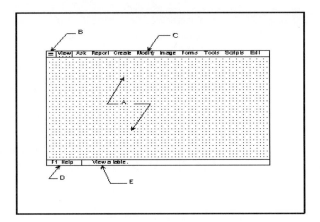

A. _____

_____

B. _____

_____

C. _____

_____

D. _____

_____

E. _____

_____

## EXERCISE 4

### PRACTICING OPENING FILES

The following topics assume that you know how to load Paradox, change the default drive, and open files. No further instructions are supplied for these procedures.

To make sure that you know how to perform the operations, open the CUSTHOLD, PURCHOLD, EMPLHOLD, and TIMEHOLD files using VIEW from the menu bar.

# Executing Commands

**After completing this topic, you will be able to:**
- Select commands from the Paradox menu bar
- Display on-line help with the HELP command
- Select a topic from the Help Index
- List most frequently used Paradox shortcut keys

Unlike most database programs, Paradox operates completely from a series of menus. All you need to do is select a command from the menu bar (using the keyboard or the mouse), and respond to the information that appears on your screen. You do not need to memorize any commands, and if you forget any details, you can always press [F1] for on-line help. Paradox's help is *context-sensitive*, which means that the help you access directly relates to the task you are performing at the time you request help.

## ► P A R A D O X    T U T O R I A L

In this tutorial, you will execute commands by selecting them from the menu bar at the top of the screen. You will also explore Paradox's help system so that you can find help on commands when working on your own.

### GETTING STARTED

1. Load Paradox into the computer's memory.

### OPENING A FILE

**THE DISK TO USE**

Beginning with this tutorial, use the data disk that contains the files you copied from the original *Resource Disk* in Exercise 2 of Topic 1. If you have not completed that exercise, you must do so before you continue.

2. Place your data disk in an appropriate drive.
3. Set the default drive as follows:
   - Open the TOOLS menu and choose More.
   - Choose Directory from the next menu.
   - When the dialog box appears, type **A:** (or **B:**, depending on which drive contains your data disk) in the text box and press [Enter ←].
4. Open the VIEW menu and press [Enter ←] or click on OK.
   - Use the arrow keys or the mouse to select OVERVIEW from the list of files and press [Enter ←] again.

**A Typical VIEW Window**

When you are using Paradox version 4.0 you will spend much of your time working in a window that is similar to this.

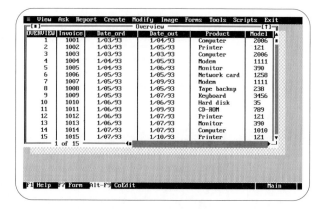

## EXPLORING HELP

5. Press [F1] to display the initial Paradox help screen.

**The Initial Help Screen**

This is the first screen you will see when you select help ([F1]).

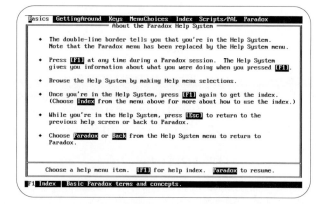

6. Press [F1] again and the Help Index is displayed.

7. Press [PgDn] and [PgUp] to scroll through help screen topics.

8. Press [Home] to return to the top of the Help Index.

9. Highlight a topic that interests you, and press [Enter←] to display details about that topic. When you are finished reading, press [F1] to redisplay the Help Index.

10. Continue experimenting on your own until you are comfortable using the help system. Commands that you can use are always listed at the bottom of the screen.

11. When you are finished, press [Esc] until you return to the main Paradox screen.

12. Open the TOOLS menu and press [F1]. Additional information about the TOOLS menu is displayed.

**The TOOLS Help Screen**
This is the screen that you will see if you request help about the TOOLS menu.

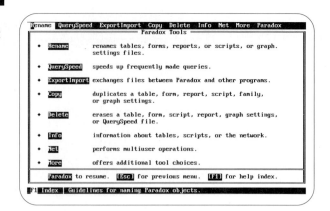

13. When you are finished, press [Esc] to return to the main Paradox screen.
14. Open the IMAGE menu and press [F1]. Additional information about the IMAGE menu is displayed.
15. Press [Esc] to return to the main Paradox screen.
16. Press [F1] twice. The Help Index is displayed.
17. Press [Ctrl]-[Z] to open the Zoom window.
18. Type **DIRECTORY** in the Value box and press [Enter←]. Paradox searches the list of topics and highlights the Directory entry. To read this entry, press [Enter←].
19. Press [Esc] until you return to the main Paradox screen.

**FINISHING UP**

20. Press [Alt]-[F8] to clear the desktop and close all files that are open.
21. You have completed this tutorial. Either go on to the next activity or (if you are finished), exit the program. If you exit the program, remove your disks and turn off the computer.

# ▶ Q U I C K   R E F E R E N C E

## PARADOX SHORTCUT KEYS

| Key | Command |
| --- | --- |
| [F1] | HELP |
| [F2] | DO_IT! |
| [Ctrl]-[F4] | Next Window |
| [Shift]-[F5] | Toggle window size |
| [Alt]-[F7] | Instant report |
| [F8] | Clear image |
| [Ctrl]-[F8] | Close the active window |
| [Alt]-[F8] | Clear All |
| [F9] | Edit |
| [F10] | Menu |

All commands in Paradox are selected from menus. Just use the mouse or the keyboard to select the command that you need. Help text displays whenever you press [F1].

The table "Paradox Shortcut Keys" lists the functions of some of the other keys that Paradox uses.

## EXERCISE 1

### EXPLORING HELP

Load Paradox. When the main screen appears, press F1 twice to display the Help Index screen. Press Ctrl-Z, type the name of the first topic listed below, then press Enter↵ twice. Summarize the displayed information about that topic in the space provided. When you are finished, press F1 to return to the Help Index screen. Repeat this procedure for each topic in the list.

ARROW KEYS _____

_____

_____

_____

CLEAR ALL KEY _____

_____

_____

_____

CONTROL KEYS _____

_____

_____

_____

DESKTOP _____

_____

_____

_____

## EXERCISE 2

### LOCATING COMMANDS ON THE MENU BAR

Follow the command sequence to locate each of the commands listed below. After locating each command, press F1 (while the menu is open), and write down a brief description of what each command is used for.

### MENU CHOICES

| Command | Function |
|---|---|
| TOOLS-MORE-DIRECTORY | _____ |
| TOOLS-MORE-EMPTY | _____ |
| VIEW | _____ |
| REPORT-OUTPUT | _____ |
| TOOLS-INFO-STRUCTURE | _____ |
| MODIFY-SORT | _____ |

# REVIEW

- A database is one or more files that contain an organized body of data.
- To create and use a database, you use a record management program or a database management program. Record management programs can work with only one file at a time. Database management programs can work with two or more files at the same time.
- Paradox is a relational database program, which means that it stores data in tables. These tables can be related to one another so you can work with more than one at a time.
- Fields are individual pieces of information such as a telephone number, a first name, a street address, or a price.
- Records are collections of fields that describe a person, thing, or activity.
- To work with a database file, you must first open the file. This copies the data from the file on the disk into the computer's memory. When using Paradox, you open files from the VIEW menu.
- To change the default drive and path with Paradox, open the TOOLS menu, choose More, then Directory, and type the name of the drive and the path in the text box that appears.
- To list database files on the disk, open the VIEW menu, type the name of the drive and the path (if necessary), and press [Enter ←].
- To print the records in a file quickly, you can use press [Alt]-[F7].
- To remove files from memory, press [Alt]-[F8] (which is called *Clear All*).
- To quit Paradox, open the EXIT menu, and select Yes.
- To display the help menu, press [F1]. For help on a specific topic, press [F1] a second time to display the Help Index.
- The help in Paradox is "context sensitive." In other words, anytime you press [F1], Paradox displays a help topic that directly relates to what you are doing at that time.

# CHAPTER 1

# QUESTIONS

## FILL IN THE BLANK

1. The main difference between a database management program and a record management program is that the database management program can work with ___two or more___ file.
2. When a table is displayed you can press ___Alt - F7___ to print it.
3. The individual pieces of data that make up a record are called ___Fields___.

4. To open a Paradox file named PAYROLL, you would use the _____*View*_____ menu.
5. To change the default drive to drive A, you would use the _*Tools–More–Directory*_ menu.
6. To list the database files on the disk, you would use the _____*View=name=↵*_____ menu.
7. To close all open files, press _*F8 or Alt–F8*_.
8. To quit Paradox, you open the _____*Exit*_____ menu.
9. To display the Help Index, press _____*F1*_____ twice.
10. To display specific help on the VIEW menu, open the menu and press _____*F1*_____.

## MATCH THE COLUMNS

| | |
|---|---|
| 1. Record management program | _4_ Opens a database file |
| 2. Database management program | _9_ A description of a person or thing |
| 3. EXIT command | _5_ Removes databases from memory |
| 4. VIEW command | _11_ A database that organizes data into tables |
| 5. CLEAR ALL command | _1_ A program that can only work with a single file |
| 6. Relational database | _6_ One or more files of related information |
| 7. Record file | _2_ A program that can work with multiple files |
| 8. Field | _3_ Command to exit the program |
| 9. Record | _10_ Displays the help menu |
| 10. [F1] | _7_ A single file (as opposed to a database) |
| 11. Database | _8_ One part of a record |
| 12. [Esc] | _12_ Cancels a selection |

## WRITE OUT THE ANSWERS

1. Define the term *database*.
2. Explain the main difference between a record management program and a database management program.
3. What are two or three disadvantages to using a record management program instead of a database management program?
4. What is a database model? Which model is most frequently used for programs that run on microcomputers?
5. What are columns and rows called when discussed in the context of a relational database table?
6. What is a field? A record? Give examples of each.
7. List the steps you would follow to start the Paradox program on your system.
8. To display the initial Paradox help screen, what key would you press?

9.  When you want to quit a Paradox session, what task must you perform before you do so? Why?

10. How do you select a choice from a pull-down menu?

# P R O J E C T S

## PROJECT 1

### EXPLORING THE TITLES DATABASE

The *Resource Disk* contains a file named TITLHOLD. This file contains a listing of the titles in a book publisher's catalog. The file contains the ISBN (a unique number assigned by the publisher in cooperation with the Library of Congress to each book that is published) along with the book's title, author, edition, version, list price, and the category in which the publisher places it. Open this file, list its records on the screen, then print the list.

## PROJECT 2

### EXPLORING THE SALES DATABASE

The *Resource Disk* contains a file named SALEHOLD. This file contains the sales in various markets for the titles listed in the TITLHOLD file. Open this file and list its records. Print the list.

# Creating & Editing Database Files

## Defining a Database File's Structure

**After completing this topic, you will be able to:**
■ Explain how to plan a database
■ Define a database file with the CREATE command
■ Describe the different types of fields
■ Print out a file's structure

As you plan a database, think backwards. Before you start, think about the questions that your data will need to answer. With that in mind, the number of fields you set up depends on the amount of data you want to store and how you want to manipulate it. For example, if you use only one field for both first and last names, then enter names like Patrick Henry, George Washington, and Betsy Ross, your file will be limited because you will not be able to sort your file based on last names. In some cases, you might not even be able to find a particular record. To avoid this, you can set up two fields: one for first names and one for last names. The same principle applies to all of the fields in your database. For example, if you do not enter zip codes in a separate field, you will not be able to sort records by zip code.

Designing a relational database requires very careful planning because it can contain two or more interrelated tables of data. Ideally, each table should have a field that contains data that is used as a unique identifier for each record. If two or more tables have the same identifying fields, these fields can be used to link the tables for many operations. Fields that contain data such as last names will normally not suffice for this purpose. If the database gets large enough, there will almost certainly be duplicate names. For example, if there are two or more "Jones" in your database, then that data is no longer a unique identifier. Many kinds of data can be used to uniquely identify records. For example:

■ Social security numbers
■ Part numbers
■ Serial numbers
■ Vehicle license numbers
■ Driver's license numbers

- Bank account numbers
- Dates and times
- Customer account numbers
- Employee serial numbers
- Purchase order numbers
- Telephone numbers
- Credit card numbers
- Policy numbers

**The Database Plan**

When you plan a database, select a name, a type, and a width (or length) for each field. If you want to be able to join one database with another, both databases must have one field that is common to both files. For example, in this database, there are two files. One lists customer names and addresses; the other records any purchases. The common field is the ID number field.

```
2/14/93   Standard Report    Page   1


Field Name                    Field Type
--------------------------    ---------
Id #                          A3
Last name                     A10
First name                    A10
Street                        A17
City                          A10
ST                            A2
Zip                           A5
Area                          A3
Phone                         A8
Date                          D
Age                           N
Remarks                       M10
```

**The Structure for the CUSTOMER Database.**

```
2/14/93    Standard Report     Page   1


Field Name                    Field Type
--------------------------    ---------
Id #                          A3
Date                          D
Item Description              A25
Amount                        $
Payment Method                A5
```

**The Structure for the PURCHASE Database.**

---

### PARADOX TUTORIAL

A recent college graduate who was interested in unique toys decided to open a business called Alice's Wonderland. As a manager, she soon realized that she needed a database to store the names and addresses of customers. Her plan was to use this database to prepare mailings for special events and sales. In this tutorial, you will define the CUSTOMER database file and use it to store names, addresses, and other information for Alice's store.

### GETTING STARTED

1. Load Paradox. Set the default drive to the one that contains your data disk.

### CREATING A NEW FILE

2. Open the CREATE menu. Type **CUSTOMER** in the text box, and press Enter⏎ . After a brief pause, the screen that is used to define a database file appears.
   - The left-hand side of the screen is divided into three columns that are used to define fields. The cursor is located (blinking) in the column with the heading *Field Name*.
   - The right-hand side of the screen displays a short description of each of the field types available.

---

**GETTING OUT OF TROUBLE**

Before proceeding, review the following ways for getting out of trouble:
- Press F1 to display help.
- Press Esc to cancel commands.
- Press ← Bksp to delete characters to the left of the cursor if you make a mistake when entering commands or data.

**The Empty CREATE Screen**
When you begin to design your database, the screen will look like this.

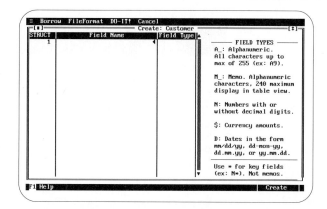

## DEFINING THE FILE

3.  When you start to define a database file, the cursor should be on the left side of the second column. The number (1) in the left column indicates which field you are defining. To enter field definitions, refer to the table "The CUSTOMER File Structure" and follow these procedures:

    ■ **Field Names.** Type a name for the field and press Enter ← to move the cursor into the Field Type column. Each field name must be unique. It can be up to 25 characters long (including spaces) but cannot contain any of the following:

    - A space at the beginning of the field name
    - Brackets [ ], braces { }, double quotes ", or parentheses ( )
    - The # all by itself
    - The character combination ->

    ■ **Field Types.** A field type is selected by typing a single letter. For additional information on field types, refer to the Quick Reference at the end of this topic.

    - If you are defining an Alphanumeric field, type **A** followed by a number that indicates the maximum length of the data (up to 255 characters).
    - To select a Memo field, type **M** followed by a number that indicates the maximum length of the data that will be displayed. (Note: A Memo field can be up to 64 megabytes in length. The number you specify here does not affect the length of the Memo; it only controls the way that it displays in a table view.)
    - If you need a Numeric field, type **N**. Paradox automatically assigns the maximum length.
    - Select a Currency field by typing **$** (dollar sign). Paradox treats a currency field just like a numeric field, except it will display with commas and automatically round off to two decimal places.
    - To define a Date field, type **D**.

    ■ When you select Numeric, Currency, or Date fields, Paradox automatically sets the field width.

> **NOTE**
>
> Paradox has three additional field types known as *Short Number Fields, Binary Fields* and *Unknown.* However, these field types are beyond the scope of this tutorial.

## THE CUSTOMER FILE STRUCTURE

| Field | Field Name | Type / Width |
|-------|------------|--------------|
| 1 | Id # | A3 |
| 2 | Last name | A10 |
| 3 | First name | A10 |
| 4 | Street | A17 |
| 5 | City | A10 |
| 6 | ST | A2 |
| 7 | Zip | A5 |
| 8 | Area | A3 |
| 9 | Phone | A8 |
| 10 | Date | D |
| 11 | Age | N |
| 12 | Remarks | M10 |

Carefully check your entries against the figure "The Completed CUSTOMER File Structure." If you find an error in your definitions, move the cursor to the error and correct it.

**The Completed CUSTOMER File Structure**
When you have finished defining your database, your screen should look like this. If there are any differences between your screen and the one shown here, make corrections before you continue.

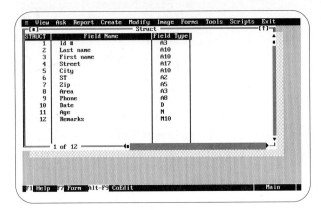

4. Select DO-IT! to save your new file. Paradox returns to the desktop.

5. Now you are ready to enter data into your new database. Choose MODIFY from the menu bar and when the pull-down menu appears, select DataEntry. Press [Enter ←] to see a list of the database files on the default drive, select CUSTOMER, and press [Enter ←] or click OK.

A new table is displayed. You will see your field names at the top of each column as shown in the table view of the figure "The Data Entry Screen." If you press [F7], a data entry form similar to the form view of the figure appears.

**The Data Entry Screen - Table and Form Views**

This figure shows the default Data Entry Screen and the standard report form, which is displayed when you press F7 .

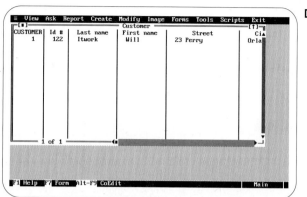

Default Data Entry Screen

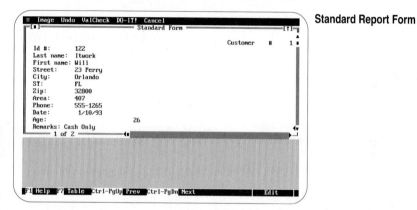

Standard Report Form

| RECORD 1 | |
|---|---|
| Id #: | 122 |
| Last Name: | Itwork |
| First Name: | Will |
| Street: | 23 Perry |
| City: | Orlando |
| ST: | FL |
| Zip: | 32800 |
| Area: | 407 |
| Phone: | 555-1265 |
| Date: | 1/10/93 |
| Age: | 26 |
| Remarks: | Cash Only |

| RECORD 2 | |
|---|---|
| Id #: | 123 |
| Last Name: | Burnem |
| First Name: | Chrispin |
| Street: | 345 Oak |
| City: | Los Gatos |
| ST: | CA |
| Zip: | 95031 |
| Area: | 415 |
| Phone: | 555-2653 |
| Date: | 02/12/93 |
| Age: | 27 |
| Remarks: | |

**Records to Add to the CUSTOMER Database**

This figure shows the two records that you should add to the CUSTOMER database.

6. Refer to the following steps and the figure "Records to Add to the CUSTOMER Database" to enter data into your file.

■ When you finish typing data into a field, press Enter ↵ to move the cursor to the beginning of the next field. If the number of characters you enter reaches the field width, the system will beep.

■ Type in the data exactly as shown in the figures. Pay attention to upper and lowercase letters because the program is case sensitive. For example, if you enter **CA** and later look for *Ca*, the program will not find it.

■ If you make a mistake when typing an entry, press ← Bksp and reenter the data correctly.

■ Date fields can contain any valid date between January 1, 100 and December 31, 9999. Leap years and leap centuries are handled automatically. For dates outside of the 20th century, you must specify a three or four digit year (yyy or yyyy). You can enter dates in one of the following formats:
  ● mm/dd/yy (as in 08/04/53)
  ● dd-Mon-yy (as in 04-Aug-53)
  ● dd.mm.yy (as in 08.04.53)
  ● yy.mm.dddd (as in 08.04.1953)

■ To type data into the Remarks field, press Alt - F5 , and the editor window opens. When you are finished, press F2 (DO_IT!), and the editor closes.

■ After you enter data in the last field, press Enter ↵ , and a new blank record is displayed.

### CHECKING AND EDITING YOUR RECORDS

7. After entering both records, use ⎯Tab⎯⇥ or the left and right arrow keys to examine your data and correct any errors that you find.

   When you are finished making corrections, exit the EDIT mode by pressing ⎯F2⎯ or choosing DO_IT! from the menu bar. Paradox automatically saves your changes.

   Carefully check your data against the figures for the two records. If you find mistakes in a record, use the arrow keys to move to the mistake, then edit it with these basic commands:

   - Press ⎯F9⎯ to activate the EDIT mode.
   - Press ⎯Ctrl⎯-⎯← Bksp⎯ to delete the entire entry, then retype it correctly.

### LISTING AND PRINTING THE FILE'S STRUCTURE AND CONTENTS

8. Open the TOOLS menu, choose Info, then Structure, and press ⎯Enter ←⎯. Select CUSTOMER from the list of files and press ⎯Enter ←⎯. A new window opens that displays the structure of your database.

**The Structure of the Completed CUSTOMER Database**

After you define the CUSTOMER database, its structure should look similar to this figure.

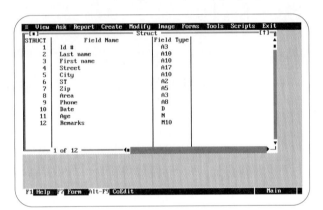

9. Select REPORT from the menu bar and choose Output from the pull-down menu. When the next window appears, press ⎯Enter ←⎯ *four* times. When the printer is finished, close the Structure window by pressing ⎯F8⎯ or click on the tiny box in the upper-left corner of the window.

   Compare your printout with the figure "The Structure of the Completed CUSTOMER Database" and make sure they match. If your database does not match the one shown here, you will learn how to correct it in the next topic.

10. Select REPORT from the menu bar and choose Output from the pull-down menu. When the next window appears, type **A:** (or **B:**, depending on which drive contains your data disk) in the Table box and press ⎯Enter ←⎯. Select CUSTOMER from the list of files and press ⎯Enter ←⎯ *three* times.

    Compare the *data* in your report to the figures shown in the text. If your database does not match the one shown here, you'll learn how to correct it in the next topic.

    When you are finished, press ⎯Alt⎯-⎯F8⎯ to clear the Paradox work area.

**NOTE**

Different printers may produce output in slightly different formats. For example, your report may print on two pages.

## CREATING A NEW FILE

After creating the CUSTOMER file to store member names and addresses, Alice decided to create a file in which to store her customer's purchases. Since she is using a relational database, she does not need to enter names and addresses into this new file if it contains a field that lists customers' ID numbers.

Charges logged into the new file by ID number can be linked to the customer's name and address in the CUSTOMER file whenever bills or statements are prepared.

11. Open the CREATE menu.
12. Type **PURCHASE** in the Table box and press [Enter⏎]. The screen that is used to define a file appears.

## DEFINING THE FILE

13. When you start to define a database file, the cursor should be on the left side of the second column. The number (1) in the left column indicates which field you are defining. To enter field definitions, refer to the table "The PURCHASE File Structure".

## THE PURCHASE FILE STRUCTURE

| Field | Field Name | Type / Width |
|-------|------------|--------------|
| 1 | Id # | A3 |
| 2 | Date | D |
| 3 | Item Description | A25 |
| 4 | Amount | $ |
| 5 | Payment Method | A5 |

Carefully check your entries against the figure "The Completed PURCHASE File Structure." If you find an error in your definition, move the cursor to the error and correct it.

**The Completed PURCHASE File Structure**
When you have finished defining the PURCHASE database, your screen should look like this.

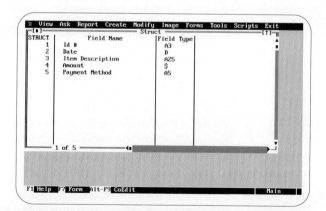

14. Press [F2] to save your new file's structure.
15. To enter data into the file, choose MODIFY from the menu bar. When the pull-down menu appears, select DataEntry. Press [Enter⏎] to see a list of the database files on the default drive, select PURCHASE, and press [Enter⏎] or click OK. Refer to the figure

**RECORD 1**

| Id #: | 122 |
|---|---|
| Date: | 04/10/93 |
| Item Description: | White Rabbit (back order) |
| Amount: | 29.95 |
| Payment Method: | Cash |

**RECORD 2**

| Id #: | 123 |
|---|---|
| Date: | 04/19/92 |
| Item Description: | Chess board |
| Amount: | 39.95 |
| Payment Method: | Check |

**Records to Add to the PURCHASE Database**
This figure shows the two records that you should add to the PURCHASE database.

**Printout of the New PURCHASE Database**

"Records to Add to the PURCHASE Database" and the following steps to complete your entries.

- After you complete a field entry, press Enter↵ to move the cursor to the beginning of the next field.
- Enter dates in the format mm/dd/yy.
- When you enter numbers, you can type . (the period) to identify the decimal point.
- After you type data in the last field of a record and press Enter↵, the cursor automatically moves to the next record.

16. Carefully check your data against the figures. If you find mistakes in a record, use the arrow keys to move to the field in error, use ← Bksp to delete the error, then retype the correct data. After entering both records, press F2 to exit and save your file.

## LISTING AND PRINTING THE FILE'S CONTENTS

17. Select REPORT from the menu bar and choose Output from the pull-down menu. When the next window appears, press Enter↵. Select PURCHASE from the list of files and press Enter↵ *three* times. Compare your printout with the figures in the text. If your database does not match the one shown here, you'll learn how to correct it in the next topic.

```
3/28/93                    Standard Report                         Page

ID#   Date      Item Description          Amount        Payment Method
----  -------   ------------------------  ----------    --------------
122   4/10/93   White Rabbit (back order)     29.95     Cash
123   4/19/93   Chess Board                   39.95     Check
```

## FINISHING UP

18. You have completed this tutorial. Press Alt - F8 to clear the desktop and close any files that might be open. Go on to the next activity or exit the program.

---

# QUICK REFERENCE

When you define a database, you specify each field's name, type, width, and decimal places, if any.

### Defining a Database
To define a database file, open the CREATE menu, type a filename in the text box and press Enter↵. After a brief pause, the screen that is used to define a database file appears.

### CREATE DATABASE COMMANDS

| To | Use this Command |
|---|---|
| Move the Cursor | Press Enter↵ or use the arrow keys |
| Delete Characters | Press ← Bksp |
| Insert a record | Press Ins |
| Delete a record | Press Del |
| Exit without saving the file | Choose CANCEL from the menu bar |

*Field Names*

When naming fields in a database file, observe the following rules:

- A field name cannot be used twice in the same file.
- Field names must be between one and twenty-five characters long (including spaces) and cannot contain any of the following:
  - A space at the beginning of the field name
  - Brackets [ ], braces { }, double quotes ", or parentheses ( )
  - The # by itself
  - The character combination ->

*Field Types*

Paradox lets you store characters, numbers, currency dates, and comments. Each of these types of data has a corresponding field type.

- ***Alphanumeric fields*** store all characters you can enter from the keyboard, including letters, numbers, symbols, and spaces. When data such as zip codes or telephone numbers are entered into a character field, they are treated as text, not values. Numbers entered in character fields cannot be used in calculations, but can have leading zeros, such as those used in the zip code 01945.
- ***Numeric fields*** store values, including numbers, signs, and decimals up to 15 significant digits. Numbers entered in these fields can be used in calculations. Data in these fields cannot have leading zeros.
- ***Date fields*** store dates, which can then be used in calculations. For example, you can add or subtract dates, or add or subtract numbers to or from them. This allows you to get answers to questions like "What is the average number of days between orders?"
- ***Memo fields*** store general descriptive text. A single memo field can be up to 64 megabytes in length, but in the Table View, you can only see a maximum of 240 characters.
- ***Currency fields*** are just like numeric fields except they display numbers rounded to two decimals places and always include whole number separators. For example, the number 1000000 would display as 1,000,000 in a currency field.

*Field Widths*

Paradox automatically sets the widths of the Date, Numeric, and Currency fields, but you must specify the width of Alphanumeric and Memo fields. The field widths that Paradox allows are listed in the table "Paradox Field Widths."

Determining field widths is a task that deserves a bit of serious thought. If you make the field too short, you will lose information. For instance, if you allowed only seven characters for a last name field, you could enter the name *Smith* but not the name *Hamilton*. But if you make the field too long, you waste storage space in the computer's memory and on your disks. Therefore, you need to balance the amount of information held against the space required to hold that information.

---

**NOTE**

Paradox also allows field types known as *Binary*, *Short Number*, and *Unknown*. However, a discussion of these fields is beyond the scope of this text.

## PARADOX FIELD WIDTHS

| Field Type | Width (in characters) |
|------------|-----------------------|
| Character fields | 1-255 |
| Numeric fields | Set automatically |
| Currency fields | Set automatically |
| Date fields | Set automatically |
| Memo fields | 1- 240 in a Table View |
|  | Up to 64 megabytes in length (set automatically) |

## Displaying a File's Structure

Open the TOOLS menu, choose Info, then Structure. Type the letter for the drive that contains your files, and press [Enter ←]. Select your file from the list and press [Enter ←]. A new window opens that displays the structure of your database.

## ► E X E R C I S E S

### THE EMPLOYEE FILE STRUCTURE

| Field Name | Type / Width |
|------------|--------------|
| Employee # | A3 |
| Last name | A10 |
| First name | A10 |
| Street | A20 |
| City | A10 |
| ST | A2 |
| Zip | A5 |
| Payrate | $ |

### EXERCISE 1

#### DEFINING A DATABASE FOR EMPLOYEES

In this exercise, you will define a database that contains information on employees. Use the table "The EMPLOYEE File Structure" to define your database.

After creating and saving the structure, make a printout of the database's structure. Compare it to the one in the figure "Printout of the EMPLOYEE Database Structure."

**Printout of the EMPLOYEE Database Structure**

```
3/28/93                 Standard Report                     Page  1


Field Name                      Field Type
----------------------------    ----------
Employee #                      A3
Last Name                       A10
First Name                      A10
Street                          A20
City                            A10
ST                              A2
Zip                             A5
Payrate                         $
```

## THE TIME FILE STRUCTURE

| Field Name | Type / Width |
|------------|--------------|
| Employee # | A3 |
| Hours | N |
| Shift | A1 |

**Printout of the TIME Database Structure**

## DEFINING A DATABASE FOR TIME KEEPING

In this exercise, you will define a database that contains data on the hours that employees worked. Use the table "The TIME File Structure" to define your database.

After creating and saving the structure, make a printout of the database's structure. Compare it to the one in the figure "Printout of the TIME Database Structure."

```
3/28/93                Standard Report                    Page

Field Name                 Field Type
---------------------------  ----------
Employee #                 A3
Hours                      N
Shift                      A1
```

# Modifying a Database File's Structure

**After completing this topic, you will be able to:**
- Modify the structure of an existing database
- Redefine existing fields in a database

After your database has been created, you may need to add, delete, or change the definition of existing fields. For example, a few years ago, many databases needed restructuring when the zip code changed from five to ten characters. If a change like this is necessary, or if fields must be added or deleted, your files can be *restructured*.

## ▶ P A R A D O X   T U T O R I A L

When you defined the CUSTOMER database file, you may have made some mistakes. In this tutorial, you retrieve a similar file and correct the file's structure.

### GETTING STARTED

1. Start Paradox and select the A (or B) drive as the default directory.
2. Open the WRONG database file.
3. Open the REPORT menu, choose Output, and print a copy of the file's contents.
4. Open the TOOLS menu, choose Info, then Structure, and press Enter←. Select the WRONG database. A window opens that displays the file's structure.
5. Open the REPORT menu again, choose Output, and print a copy of the file's structure. When the printer stops, close the Structure window.

**The Original WRONG File Structure**
When you print out the file structure for the WRONG database, it should look like the one shown here.

```
3/28/93                    Standard Report                   Page 1


Field Name                      Field Type
---------------------------     ----------
Id                              A3
Lstname                         A10
First                           A10
Street                          A17
City                            A10
ST                              A2
Zip                             N
Phone                           A8
Enrolled                        D
Age                             N
Ages                            N
```

### CHANGING THE NAME OF A FIELD

6. Open the MODIFY menu, choose Restructure, and press [Enter ←].
   Choose WRONG from the list of files that is displayed.
7. Move the cursor to the second field where *Last name* is misspelled
   *Lst name.*
8. Use [← Bksp] to erase the entry, then retype it correctly.

### ADDING A FIELD

9. Move the cursor to field 8, *Phone.*
10. Press [Ins]. A blank field appears.
11. Enter its name as *Area*, and select a field type of A3.

### DELETING A FIELD

12. Move the cursor to field 12, *Age.*
13. Press [Del]. The field disappears.

### CHANGING A FIELD'S TYPE

14. Move the cursor to record 7, *Zip.*
15. Change the type to *A5*. When you finish, your screen should look
    like the one shown in the figure "The Modified WRONG Structure."
16. Press [F2] (DO_IT!) to leave the RESTRUCTURE mode and save your
    changes.

**The Modified WRONG Structure**
After modifying the structure of the WRONG database file, its structure should look like the one shown here.

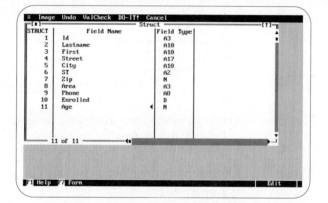

17. Paradox asks you to confirm the deletion of the *Age* field. Choose
    Delete. Paradox copies the old records into the new, restructured
    database. Note: If you delete a field accidentally, choose Oops!
    (rather than Delete) and the field is restored.

### PRINTING THE FILE'S CONTENTS AND STRUCTURE

18. Open the REPORT menu, and choose Output to print a copy of the
    file's contents.
19. Open the TOOLS menu, choose Info, then Structure, and press
    [Enter ←]. Select the WRONG database. A window opens that displays
    the file's structure.
20. Open the REPORT menu again, choose Output, and print a copy
    of the file's structure. When the printer stops, press [Alt]-[F8] to close
    all of your windows and save your file.

**FINISHING UP**

21. You have completed this tutorial. Go on to the next activity or exit the program.

## QUICK REFERENCE

To change the structure of a database, open the MODIFY menu, choose Restructure, press [Enter ←], and choose your file from the list. When you save the revised structure, Paradox copies the records back into the revised file.

When restructuring files, keep the following points in mind:

- If the restructuring adds new fields, the new fields will be blank.
- To edit an existing field, move the cursor to the field, and use [← Bksp] to make corrections.
- To insert a new field, position the cursor in the field and press [Ins]. The new field appears above the cursor position.
- To delete a field, position the cursor in the field and press [Del].

To save the revised structure, press [F2] (DO_IT!).

If you want to abandon any changes and leave the database as it was before you began, select CANCEL from the menu bar.

## EXERCISES

### EXERCISE 1

#### MODIFYING THE CUSTOMER AND PURCHASE FILE STRUCTURES

If you made any mistakes when defining the CUSTOMER and PUR-CHASE database files, use what you have learned in this topic to correct them. When you finish, print out the modified file structures.

### EXERCISE 2

#### MODIFYING THE EMPLOYEE FILE STRUCTURE

1. Open the EMPLOYEE file.
2. Modify the file structure by inserting a field named *Department* between the existing *Zip* and *Payrate* fields. Define the field as a character field with a width of two characters.
3. Save the revised structure and make a printout of it. Compare your printout to the one shown in the figure "The Modified EM-PLOYEE File Structure."

**The Modified EMPLOYEE File Structure**
After modifying the EMPLOYEE file structure, your printout should look like the one shown here.

```
4/18/93                    Standard Report                        Page

Field Name                 Field Type
--------------------------  ----------
Employee #                 A3
Last name                  A10
First name                 A10
Street                     A17
City                       A10
ST                         A2
Zip                        N
Phone                      A8
Department                 A2
Payrate                    $
```

## EXERCISE 3

### MODIFYING THE TIME FILE STRUCTURE

1. Open the TIME file.
2. Modify the file structure by adding a field named *Week of* above *Employee* # so that it is the first field in the file. Define the field as a date field.
3. Save the revised structure and make a printout of it. Compare your printout to the one shown in the figure "The Modified TIME File Structure."

**The Modified TIME File Structure**
After modifying the TIME file structure, your printout should look like the one shown here.

```
3/28/93                    Standard Report                        Page 1

Field Name                 Field Type
--------------------------  ----------
Week of                    D
Employee #                 A3
Hours                      N
Shift                      A1
```

# Entering Data into a Database File

After completing this topic, you will be able to:
- Add new records to a database file
- Append records to a database from another file with the ADD command

Unlike a paper database, you can easily change and update an electronic database. Adding records to a new database is not difficult, and later, you can add new records or change existing records to keep your information up to date. If the database file is not already open, use the VIEW command from the menu bar and locate the table that you need.

When you finish entering records, select DO-IT! from the menu bar to save your work. You can also copy records from another database with the ADD command.

Unlike a card index file, where you would want to insert the card in the proper order, the database management program adds it to the end of the file. You can enter new records one after another without worrying about their order. You will learn how to change the order of the records in a file in later topics.

## ▶ PARADOX TUTORIAL

In this tutorial, you will enter records into the CUSTOMER database file using the Edit key ( F9 ). Then, you will add records to the file from another file on the disk named CUSTHOLD using the ADD command. The reason you add the records from the other file is to save you typing time. Databases are interesting only when they are too large to take in at a glance. However, why waste lab time typing when Paradox can help you create a large file quickly and easily?

### GETTING STARTED

1. If necessary, change the default drive to A (or B):
   - Open the TOOLS menu and choose More.
   - When the next menu opens, choose Directory, and type **A:** (or **B:**) in the text box, and press Enter← .
2. Select VIEW from the menu bar and open the CUSTOMER database file.

## ADDING RECORDS

3. Press **F9** to activate the EDIT mode. Press **End** to move to the last record in the database, then press the down arrow to move to the next blank line.

**Adding Records to the CUSTOMER Database**
This is what your screen should look like when you are adding records to the CUSTOMER database.

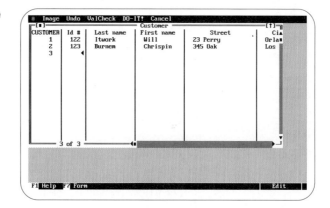

4. To enter data into the file, refer to the figure "Records to Add to the CUSTOMER Database" and the following steps.

   ■ After you complete a field entry, press **Enter ←** to move the cursor to the beginning of the next field.

   ■ Enter the data exactly as shown in the two figures. Uppercase and lowercase letters are important because when you search for data, the program is case sensitive.

   ■ If you make a mistake when typing an entry, press **← Bksp** to delete it, then reenter it correctly.

   ■ Enter dates in the format mm/dd/yy.

   ■ After entering data in the next to last field (*Age*), press **Enter ←** twice to display a new blank record.

**Records to Add to the CUSTOMER Database**
This figure shows the two records that you should add to the CUSTOMER file.

**NOTE**

If two consecutive fields have the same contents, you can save some time by pressing **Ctrl**-**D**. Paradox copies the data from the previous record into the same field of the current record. This function is called *Ditto*.

| RECORD 3 | |
|---|---|
| Id #: | 126 |
| Last Name: | Canbe |
| First Name: | Titus |
| Street: | 234 Clark |
| City: | Tampa |
| ST: | FL |
| Zip: | 33606 |
| Area: | 415 |
| Phone: | 555-2731 |
| Date: | 3/12/93 |
| Age: | 35 |
| Remarks: | |

| RECORD 4 | |
|---|---|
| Id #: | 127 |
| Last Name: | Roundalot |
| First Name: | Liza |
| Street: | 201 North Main |
| City: | Atlanta |
| ST: | GA |
| Zip: | 30010 |
| Area: | 403 |
| Phone: | 555-8764 |
| Date: | 3/5/93 |
| Age: | 89 |
| Remarks: | |

## CHECKING AND EDITING YOUR RECORDS

5. After entering both records, use the up and down arrows to scroll through them.

NOTE

It is not necessary to erase the entire entry to correct a single mistake. You can press Alt - F5 while editing and use the arrow keys (*not* ← Bksp ) to move around in your entry without erasing it. When you use Alt - F5 , you can also use Ins and Del to help make corrections.

When you finish correcting a field, press F2 (DO_IT!), then use the arrow keys to move the cursor to the next field that needs to be corrected.

**NOTE**

If you press F7 again, Paradox returns to the Standard View mode.

| RECORD 3 | |
|---|---|
| Id#: | 123 |
| Date: | 3/3/93 |
| Item Description: | Cheshire Cat (incomplete) |
| Amount: | 11.50 |
| Payment Method: | Charge |

| RECORD 4 | |
|---|---|
| Id #: | 123 |
| Date: | 3/17/93 |
| Item Description: | White Rabbit (back order) |
| Amount | 29.95 |
| Payment Method | Charge |

**Records to Add to the PURCHASE Database**
This figure shows the two records that you should add to the PURCHASE file.

Don't press down arrow if the cursor is sitting on the last line, or a new blank record will display. If this happens, press Del . The blank line disappears.

Carefully compare the two new records with the figures that you used to enter them. If you find an error, use the arrow keys to move to the mistake, use ← Bksp to delete the error, then reenter the data correctly.

### SAVING YOUR CHANGES

6. When all corrections have been made, press F2 or select DO-IT! from the menu bar.

7. When you are finished viewing your data, press Alt - F8 to clear the desktop.

### ADDING RECORDS IN THE FORM VIEW MODE

8. Select VIEW from the menu bar and open the PURCHASE database file.

9. Press F7 . Paradox changes to what is called *Form View*. When you are in this mode, Paradox displays one record at a time on what appear to be "file cards."

10. Press F9 to activate the EDIT mode. Press End to move to the last record in the database, then press PgDn . A blank form is displayed.

11. To enter data into the file, refer to the figure "Records to Add to the PURCHASE Database" and the following steps.

■ After you complete a field entry, press Enter ← to move the cursor to the beginning of the next field.

■ Enter the data exactly as shown in the two figures. Remember, uppercase and lowercase letters are important.

■ If you make a mistake when typing an entry, press ← Bksp to delete it, then reenter it correctly.

■ Enter dates in the format mm/dd/yy.

■ After entering data into the next to last field, press Enter ← . A new blank record is displayed.

12. After entering both records, use the up and down arrows to scroll through them and check for errors. When all corrections have been made, press F2 or select DO-IT! from the menu bar.

13. When you are finished viewing your data, press Alt - F8 to clear the desktop.

### APPENDING NEW RECORDS FROM ANOTHER FILE

14. Open the TOOLS menu from the menu bar and choose More. When the next menu displays, choose Add.

15. Press Enter ← (or click OK) to display a list of possible source tables. The Source table is the file that contains the records that are to be added to the old database. Choose CUSTHOLD from this list.

16. When the next window opens, choose the Target table. The Target table is the name of the old database that will receive the data from the source database. For this exercise, the Target table is the CUSTOMER database.

17. Press Enter ← (or click OK). The new records (from CUSTHOLD) are added to the CUSTOMER database.

### PRINTING THE RECORDS

18. Select REPORT from the menu bar. When the pull-down menu appears, choose Output. Select OK to display a list of files, then select the CUSTOMER table.

19. When the Report selection box appears, choose Standard Report and press Enter ← (or click OK). Select Printer (or press Enter ←) to print your database.

### FINISHING UP

20. You have completed this tutorial. Press Alt - F8 to clear the desktop and close any files that may be open. Go on to the next activity or exit the program.

## ▶ QUICK REFERENCE

### Adding Records to a Table

To enter records in a table after it has been defined, the basic command is EDIT ( F9 ). Then press End to move to the last record. Press the down arrow to start a new record. When you finish, select DO-IT! to leave the EDIT mode and save your work.

### The ADD Command

The ADD command adds records to the end of the file from any file that you specify. If the files do not have the same structure, Paradox displays a warning message. The files will not be combined.

## ▶ EXERCISES

### EXERCISE 1

#### ENTERING RECORDS INTO THE EMPLOYEE FILE

1. Open the EMPLOYEE file.
2. Enter the records shown in the figure "Records to Add to the EMPLOYEE Database."
3. When finished, save the file.
4. Add additional records to the file from EMPLHOLD. This file is on the original *Student Resource Disk* that came with this text and which you should have copied to your data disk earlier.

**Records to Add to the EMPLOYEE Database**
This figure shows the two records that you should add to the EMPLOYEE file.

| RECORD 1 | |
|---|---|
| Employee #: | 101 |
| Last Name: | Saucer |
| First Name: | Coopen |
| Street: | 400 Lewis St |
| City: | Tampa |
| ST: | FL |
| Zip: | 33606 |
| Dept: | 2 |
| Payrate: | 7.50 |

| RECORD 2 | |
|---|---|
| Employee #: | 102 |
| Last Name: | Schwartz |
| First Name: | Bermuda |
| Street: | 350 Water St. |
| City: | Tampa |
| ST: | FL |
| Zip: | 33524 |
| Dept: | 1 |
| Payrate: | 7.00 |

| RECORD 1 | |
|---|---|
| Week of: | 4/19/93 |
| Employee # | 114 |
| Hours: | 40 |
| Shift: | 1 |

| RECORD 2 | |
|---|---|
| Week of: | 4/19/93 |
| Employee #: | 115 |
| Hours: | 40 |
| Shift: | 1 |

**Records to Add to the TIME Database**
This figure shows the two records that you should add to the TIME file.

5. Print a list of the records.

## EXERCISE 2

### ENTERING RECORDS INTO THE TIME FILE

1. Open the TIME file.
2. Enter the records shown in the figure "Records to Add to the TIME Database."
3. When finished, save the file.
4. Add additional records to the file from TIMEHOLD. This file is on the original *Student Resource Disk*.
5. Print a list of the records.

## EXERCISE 3

### APPENDING RECORDS TO THE PURCHASE FILE

1. Open the PURCHASE file.
2. Add additional records to the file from PURCHOLD. This file is on the original *Student Resource Disk*.
3. When finished, save the file.
4. Print a list of the records.

# Editing & Updating Database Files

**After completing this topic, you will be able to:**
- Edit fields in EDIT mode
- Edit memo fields with [Alt]-[F5] or [Ctrl]-[F]

It is often necessary to edit or update records in a database file. For example, when an employee changes his or her address, you must change the record that stores the address. To make a change to a specific entry, you must first locate it and display it on the screen. Then, you revise the contents of the appropriate fields and save your changes.

## ▶ P A R A D O X   T U T O R I A L

In this tutorial, you will edit records in the WRONG database file. After correcting this file, you should be able to correct any mistakes you make in your own files.

### GETTING STARTED

1. If necessary, set the default drive to drive A (or B).
2. Choose VIEW from the menu bar and open the WRONG database file.

### MOVING THE CURSOR IN A TABLE

3. Press [Home] to move the cursor to the first record.
4. Press [End] to move the cursor to the last record.
5. Select IMAGE from the menu bar. When the pull-down menu appears, choose Zoom. When the next selection box appears, choose Record, then type **3** in the text box. Press [Enter←┘] (or click OK). The cursor moves to the specified record.

### EDITING RECORDS

6. Move the cursor to record 1 and press [F9] to enter the EDIT mode. Compare record 1 to the first line of the figure "The Edited WRONG File." The fields that appear in bold type may need to be changed in your file. Move the cursor to the field and press [Alt]-[F5] (or double click inside the field). Make any necessary corrections and press [Enter←┘]. When you finish, your screen should contain the same data as the figure shown here.

| ID | LASTNAME | FIRST | STREET | CITY | ST | ZIP | AREA | PHONE | ENROLLED | AGE |
|----|----------|-------|--------|------|----|----|------|-------|----------|-----|
| 222 | **Culman** | Tina | 100 Elm Street | New Haven | CT | 10000 | **203** | 555-1001 | 01/16/94 | 33 |
| 111 | **Benjamin** | Nancy | 25 Oak Street | Cambridge | MA | 20000 | **617** | 555-1002 | **01/08/94** | 26 |
| 116 | Kendall | Liz | 14 Lark Avenue | Chicago | IL | 20000 | **312** | 555-1003 | 02/02/94 | **19** |
| 120 | Hogan | Dennis | **40 Main Street** | Edgewater | NJ | 30000 | **201** | 555-1004 | 09/06/94 | 39 |
| 119 | Morin | Emily | 43 Spruce Road | Milpitas | CA | 20000 | **408** | 555-1005 | 08/01/94 | **17** |
| 333 | Sobel | Carol | 45 Porter Avenue | Fairlawn | NJ | 30000 | **201** | 555-1006 | 03/06/94 | 34 |
| 112 | Anthony | William | 900 Maple Road | **Reading** | MA | 20000 | **617** | 555-1007 | 01/07/94 | 63 |
| 118 | Morin | Cathy | 5 Milk Street | Salem | OR | 40000 | **508** | 555-1008 | **06/03/94** | 22 |
| 114 | Morin | Mike | 5 Milk Street | Salem | OR | 40000 | **508** | 555-1009 | 01/10/94 | 45 |
| 121 | **Dougherty** | Steve | 1 Sylvan Ave | Englewood | NJ | **33012** | **415** | 555-1010 | 10/15/94 | 25 |

**The Edited WRONG File**

This figure shows the WRONG file after all corrections have been made. The fields in bold may need to be changed in your file, which should match this one when you are finished.

7. Press the down arrow to move to the next record and edit it if necessary. Remember, press [Alt]-[F5] (or double click) before you make any changes to a field.

8. Repeat Steps 6 and 7 until all records are edited.

9. When you finish making corrections, select DO-IT! (or press [F2]) to save your changes.

**EDITING MEMO FIELDS**

10. Open the CUSTOMER file. Select VIEW from the menu bar, locate the file in the list, and select it. Press [Enter ↵] (or click OK) to open the table.

11. Move the cursor to the second record.

12. Move the cursor to the *Remarks* field.

13. Press [F9] to activate the EDIT mode.

14. Press [Alt]-[F5] to display the contents of the *Remarks* field (which should be empty).

15. Type **Standing order for Gum Ball machines** in the box that is displayed.

> **HINT**
>
> You can press [Ins] to select the OVERWRITE mode as you make changes to a field. When you select the OVERWRITE mode, any new data that you type replaces the old data. In other words, OVERWRITE lets you replace existing data in a single step.

**The MEMO Field Editor**

When you move the cursor to a Memo field and press [Alt]-[F5], the Memo Editor Screen is displayed.

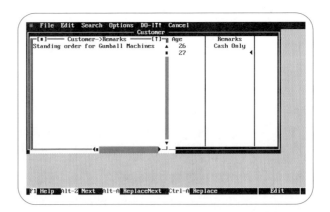

**CUSTOMER MEMO FIELD REVISIONS**

| ID | Memo Field Entry |
|----|------------------|
| 119 | Collects dolls |
| 121 | Will usually buy any "magical" items |
| 114 | Cash only-No checks |

16. When you finish, select DO-IT! (or press [F2]).

17. Write down the record numbers (listed under CUSTOMER in the first column) for the records listed in the table "CUSTOMER Memo Field Revisions." For each of those fields, repeat Steps 13 through 15, but enter the data shown in the table.

18. Press [F2] again to leave the EDIT mode and save your changes.

## PRINTING THE RECORDS

19. Open the REPORT menu from the menu bar, choose Output, and press [Enter←] (or click OK) to display a list of files. Select the revised CUSTOMER database and print a Standard report. Notice that only a small part of each memo field prints out.

20. Print the contents of the memo attached to the record with the Id number 121. Move the cursor to the Memo field for this record and press [Alt]-[F5] to display its contents. Select FILE from the menu bar. When the pull-down menu appears, choose Print. The entire contents of the Memo field is printed.

**Printing MEMO Fields**
When the contents of a Memo field is displayed, you can print it on your printer.

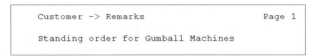

```
Customer -> Remarks                      Page 1

Standing order for Gumball Machines
```

## FINISHING UP

21. You have completed this tutorial. Press [Alt]-[F8] to clear the desktop and close any files that might be open. Go on to the next activity or exit the program.

---

# ► QUICK REFERENCE

To modify or correct existing records, activate the EDIT mode by pressing [F9]. Next, use the arrow keys to move the cursor to the desired record and field. Finally, press [Alt]-[F5] and make your changes.

## Moving to a Specific Record
When you want to move the cursor to a specific record, select IMAGE from the menu bar. When the pull-down menu appears, choose Zoom. Choose Record, type the number of the record that you need, then press [Enter←] (or click OK).

## Moving the Cursor
When Paradox displays a record for editing, the commands that you use to move the cursor around the screen are described in the table "Moving the Cursor in EDIT Mode."

### MOVING THE CURSOR IN EDIT MODE

| To move to | Press |
|---|---|
| First record | [Home] |
| Last record | [End] |
| Next field | [Enter←], [Tab⇆], or [→] |
| Previous field | [⇧ Shift]-[Tab⇆] or [←] |
| One record up or down | [↑] or [↓] |
| Next or previous screen page | [PgDn] or [PgUp] |

## Editing Fields

When you are editing records, you can use the commands shown in the table "Editing Commands." Remember, to edit a field, move the cursor to the field to be changed and press [Alt]-[F5].

### EDITING COMMANDS

| To | Press |
|---|---|
| Turn OVERTYPE mode on or off | [Ins] |
| Delete character that cursor is under | [Del] |
| Delete character to left of cursor | [← Bksp] |
| Save changes | [F2] or select **DO-IT!** |

## Editing Memo Fields

Memo fields have their own editing commands. To edit a Memo field, move the cursor to the field and press [Alt]-[F5] or [Ctrl]-[F] to display the field in Text Editing mode. The available editing commands are listed below.

### EDITING COMMANDS

| To | Press |
|---|---|
| Turn insert mode on or off | [Ins] |
| Delete current character or highlighted area | [Del] |
| Delete highlighted area or character to left of cursor | [← Bksp] |
| Delete from cursor position to end of word | [Alt]-[D] |
| Delete entire line at cursor position | [Ctrl]-[Y] |
| Copy highlighted text to clipboard | [Ctrl]-[Ins] |
| Cut highlighted text to clipboard | [⇧ Shift]-[Del] |
| Paste contents of clipboard at cursor position | [⇧ Shift]-[Ins] |
| Save changes | [F2] or select **DO-IT!** |

## ► E X E R C I S E S

### EXERCISE 1

### EDITING THE CUSTOMER AND PURCHASE FILES

If you made any mistakes when entering the records in the CUSTOMER and PURCHASE database files, use what you have learned in this topic to correct them. After doing so, print out the edited records.

---

## EXERCISE 2

---

### EDITING THE EMPLOYEE AND TIME FILES

If you made any mistakes when entering the records in the EMPLOYEE
and TIME database files, use what you have learned in this topic to
correct them. After doing so, print out the edited records.

T O P I C    7    *Deleting Records from a Database File*

> **After completing this topic, you will be able to:**
> - Remove records from your database
> - Retrieve deleted records during an editing session
> - Recover lost disk space after deleting files

Eventually, some of the information in your database will not be needed any longer. In many cases you can solve this problem simply by editing existing records. However, if a product is discontinued or an employee leaves the company, it may be necessary to delete an entire record. Deleting records in Paradox is quick, but remember, when you delete a record, it is gone forever. Always make careful decisions about what to delete from your files.

## ▶ P A R A D O X    T U T O R I A L

In this tutorial, you will delete records from the WRONG database file.

**GETTING STARTED**

1. If necessary, set the default drive to drive A (or B).
2. Select VIEW from the menu bar and open the WRONG database file.
3. Select REPORT from the menu bar and print a copy of the records in the WRONG database.

| ID | LASTNAME | FIRST | STREET | CITY | ST | ZIP | AREA | PHONE | ENROLLED | AGE |
|-----|----------|--------|-----------------|------------|----|-------|------|----------|----------|-----|
| **222** | **Culman** | **Tina** | **100 Elm Street** | **New Haven** | **CT** | **10000** | **203** | **555-1001** | **01/16/94** | **33** |
| **111** | **Benjamin** | **Nancy** | **25 Oak Street** | **Cambridge** | **MA** | **20000** | **617** | **555-1002** | **01/08/94** | **26** |
| 116 | Kendall | Liz | 14 Lark Avenue | Chicago | IL | 20000 | 312 | 555-1003 | 02/02/94 | 19 |
| **120** | **Hogan** | **Dennis** | **40 Main Street** | **Edgewater** | **NJ** | **30000** | **201** | **555-1004** | **09/06/94** | **39** |
| 119 | Morin | Emily | 43 Spruce Road | Milpitas | CA | 20000 | 408 | 555-1005 | 08/01/94 | 17 |
| **333** | **Sobel** | **Carol** | **45 Porter Avenue** | **Fairlawn** | **NJ** | **30000** | **201** | **555-1006** | **03/06/94** | **34** |
| 112 | Anthony | William | 900 Maple Road | Reading | MA | 20000 | 617 | 555-1007 | 01/07/94 | 63 |
| 118 | Morin | Cathy | 5 Milk Street | Salem | OR | 40000 | 508 | 555-1008 | 06/03/94 | 22 |
| 114 | Morin | Mike | 5 Milk Street | Salem | OR | 40000 | 508 | 555-1009 | 01/10/94 | 45 |
| 121 | Dougherty | Steve | 1 Sylvan Ave | Englewood | NJ | 33012 | 415 | 555-1010 | 10/15/94 | 25 |

**Deleting Records from the WRONG File**
In this tutorial, you will delete the boldfaced records from the WRONG database file.

**DELETING RECORDS**

4. Press F9 to activate the EDIT mode.

5. Move the cursor to record 2, and press ⌈Del⌉. Record 2 disappears. The remaining records are automatically renumbered to reflect the change. In other words, record 3 is now record 2.

6. Move the cursor to the record that is now listed as number 7. Press ⌈Del⌉ to delete it, also. Notice that the cursor can be in any field of the record when you press ⌈Del⌉ to delete the entire line (record). Once again, the remaining records are automatically renumbered.

7. Press ⌈Ctrl⌉-⌈U⌉ (for *Undo*). Record 7 reappears. Paradox automatically renumbers the list. You will also see a message at the bottom of the screen that reads: "Record 7 reinserted."

8. Press ⌈Ctrl⌉-⌈U⌉ again. Record 2 reappears. You will see the message "Record 2 reinserted."

9. Press ⌈F2⌉ (DO-IT!) to leave the EDIT mode.

    **Warning!** When you press ⌈F2⌉ (DO-IT!), any deleted records are *permanently* removed from your database. Once this happens, if you need to recover the data in a deleted record, you must reenter it as a new record.

10. Press ⌈F9⌉ to activate the EDIT mode again.

11. Move the cursor to record 2, and press ⌈Del⌉. Record 2 disappears. The remaining records are automatically renumbered.

12. Move the cursor to what is now record 5, and press ⌈Del⌉. Record 5 disappears.

13. Move the cursor to what is now record 3, and press ⌈Del⌉. Record 3 disappears.

14. Move the cursor to what is now record 1, and press ⌈Del⌉. Record 1 disappears.

15. Press ⌈F2⌉ (DO-IT!) to leave the EDIT mode. Remember, when you press ⌈F2⌉ (DO-IT!) the records that have been deleted are permanently removed from your file.

16. Select REPORT from the menu bar and print out the remaining records. When you are finished, press ⌈Alt⌉-⌈F8⌉ to clear the desktop and close any files that might be open.

### RECOVERING DISK SPACE AFTER DELETING RECORDS

When you delete records from your database, Paradox does not release the disk space that your file was using. If your database is small and you do not delete records often, this is not really a problem. However, if your database is large and is updated frequently, you might eventually run out of disk space. Use the following procedure to recover disk space that your file no longer needs.

17. Open the TOOLS menu. When the pull-down menu appears, choose Copy.

18. Select Table from the next list and press ⌈Enter ←⌉. Press ⌈Enter ←⌉ again to list the files. Choose WRONG from the list of files and press ⌈Enter ←⌉ (or click OK).

19. When the next small window opens, type **WRONG-2** in the text box. Press ⌈Enter ←⌉ or click OK.

    You have now made a backup copy of the WRONG database (named WRONG-2). If the computer or your disk malfunctions, you will not lose your work.

If a malfunction were to occur, you should delete WRONG from your disk, return to Step 17, copy the table named WRONG-2 back into WRONG, then continue.

20. Select MODIFY from the menu bar. When the pull-down menu appears, choose Restructure.

21. Press [Enter ←] (or click OK) and select the WRONG database from the list that appears.

22. When the Restructure window opens, press [F2] (DO-IT!). Paradox copies the existing database into a new database with the same name. Press [Alt]-[F8] to clear the desktop.

23. Select TOOLS from the menu bar. When the pull-down menu appears, select Delete.

24. If everything worked correctly and no error messages were displayed, choose TABLE from the next menu, press [Enter ←] (or click OK), and select the WRONG-2 file from the list that appears. Press [Enter ←] or click OK.

25. A warning message appears near the bottom of the screen. Read this message and make sure that WRONG-2 is the file that Paradox intends to delete. If everything is correct, select OK. WRONG-2 is permanently removed from your disk.

### FINISHING UP

26. You have completed this tutorial. Press [Alt]-[F8] to close all open files and clear your desktop. Go on to the next activity or, if you are finished, exit the program.

## ▶ Q U I C K    R E F E R E N C E

Paradox does not permanently delete records from the disk when you press [Del]. When you finish deleting records, press [F2] (DO-IT!) to permanently remove the records.

### Deleting Records

Begin by pressing [F9] to activate the EDIT mode. Next, move the cursor to the line that contains the record that you want to delete and press [Del]. The selected record disappears and Paradox automatically renumbers the remaining records. If you need to "undelete" a record, press [Ctrl]-[U]. The records reappear in reverse order of their deletion.

When you are ready to permanently remove the deleted records, press [F2] (or select DO-IT!). Paradox permanently deletes the records and exits from the EDIT mode.

### Recovering "Lost" Disk Space

When you delete records from your database, Paradox does not release the disk space that your file was using. To recover disk space, make a backup copy of your file, select MODIFY (from the menu bar), and restructure your file. If everything works correctly, delete the backup file. The unused disk space will be available for future use.

## Deleting All of the Records in a Database

If you ever want to delete all the records in a database, use the TOOLS-MORE-EMPTY command sequence. To perform this operation, select TOOLS from the menu bar. When the pull-down menu appears, select More. Choose Empty from the next menu and press Enter⏎ (or click OK) to display a list of files. Select the table that you want to empty, and press Enter⏎ (or click OK). You will see a warning message near the bottom of the screen. If everything is correct, press Enter⏎ (or click OK) to remove all records from the selected table.

## ➤ E X E R C I S E S

### EXERCISE 1

#### DELETING RECORDS FROM THE EMPLOYEE FILE

1. Open the EMPLOYEE file.
2. Delete the record for Employee # 104 (Justin Case).
3. Print a list of the remaining records.

### EXERCISE 2

#### DELETING RECORDS FROM THE TIME FILE

1. Open the TIME file.
2. Delete both records for Employee # 104.
3. Print a list of the remaining records.

- Planning a database is important because you want to be able to find data easily.
- To define a database file, open the CREATE menu. When the text box appears, type in a filename.
- When you define a database table, you indicate the name of the field, the type of data to be entered, and its width (number of characters).
- Field names must be unique. You cannot use the same field name more than once in a file.
- Fields that contain unique data can be used to link files.
- Field types include Alphanumeric (text), Numeric (data used for calculations), Currency (similar to numeric), Date, and Memo.
- The data entered into Memo fields can be up to 64MB in length.
- Field width is important. If a field is too short, you may lose information. If it is too long, you waste memory and disk space.
- To display a file's structure, choose TOOLS from the menu bar. When the pull-down menu appears, select Info. Next, choose Structure, locate your file, and press [Enter←] (or click OK).
- If you have an existing database, you can add, delete, or redefine fields by choosing MODIFY from the menu bar and selecting Restructure from the pull-down menu.
- To enter records into a database file, you can open the file with the VIEW command (from the menu bar) and press [F9] to activate the EDIT mode.
- You can also add records if you choose MODIFY from the menu bar and select DataEntry from the pull-down menu.
- When you press [F2] (DO-IT!), Paradox saves the records you have entered into the database.
- You can append records from another file if you choose TOOLS from the menu bar and select More, then Add from the series of pull-down menus. Finally, specify the Source table (the table that contains the records to be added) and the Target table (the "original" table) to complete the operation.
- You can move the cursor with the arrow keys, [Tab⇆], [⇧ Shift]-[Tab⇆], or by pressing [Enter←].
- You can edit a field in a record if you press [F9] (EDIT), then press [Alt]-[F5].
- You can only edit Memo fields if you move the cursor to the Memo field that you want to change and press [Alt]-[F5] or [Ctrl]-[F] while in the EDIT mode.
- You can delete records from a database in two steps. First, activate the EDIT mode by pressing [F9]. Next, move the cursor to the record that you want to delete, and press [Del].
- You can "undelete" records by pressing [Ctrl]-[U]. Records are replaced in the reverse order of their deletion.
- When you press [F2] (or select DO-IT!), all deletions and other changes become permanent changes.

# QUESTIONS

## FILL IN THE BLANK

1. A ___field___ contains unique data such as social security numbers.

2. To create a database file named CUST, you would choose the ___Create___ command from the menu bar.

3. If you want to use numbers for calculations, you must store them in a ___Numeric___ field.

4. To display the structure of an existing file, you can choose the ___Tools___ - ___Info___ - ___Structure___ command sequence from the menu bar and pull-down menus.

5. To restructure an open database file, choose the ___Modify___ - ___Restructure___ command sequence from the menu bar.

6. To add new records to the end of a database file that is already displayed on your desktop, you must first activate the ___Edity___ mode, then move the cursor to the ___Data Entry___ of the table.

7. To add new records from another file named RECADD, you would use the command ___Tools___. ___More-Add___

8. When a table is displayed on your desktop, you can use the ___Image___ - ___Zoom___ - ___←___ command sequence to move the cursor directly to a specific record number.

9. To edit the contents of a specific field, activate the EDIT mode, move the cursor to the field that you want to change, then press ___Alt - F5___. _F₃_

10. To display the contents of a memo field, activate the EDIT mode, position the cursor in the field, and press ___Alt - 5___ or ___Ctrl - F___.

11. To delete records from a database, you must first select the ___Edit___ mode.

12. To remove a record, move the cursor to the record to be removed, then press the ___Del___ key.

13. When you press ___F₂___, all deletions and other changes are permanent.

14. If you have not saved your file, you can "undelete" records by pressing ___Ctrl - U___.

## MATCH THE COLUMNS

1. Field with unique data for each record
2. CREATE command
3. Field width
4. TOOLS-INFO-STRUCTURE command sequence
5. Numeric fields

___3___ Fields with variable widths

___8___ The command sequence used to restructure a database

___12___ "Undeletes" records

___2___ Used to define the structure of a new database

___8___ Determines the number of characters that you can enter in a field

6. Date fields
7. Memo fields
8. MODIFY-RESTRUCTURE command sequence
9. TOOLS-MORE-ADD command sequence
10. The arrow keys, [Tab⇆], and [⇧ Shift]-[Tab⇆]
11. [Del]
12. [Ctrl]-[U]

_9_ The command sequence used to add records from another file

_7_ The command sequence used to list field definitions in a database file

_5_ Numbers in these fields can be calculated

_6_ Contains dates

_1_ A field that can be used to link files

_10_ Moves the cursor in a table

_11_ Removes records from a database

## WRITE OUT THE ANSWERS

1. Briefly describe each of the following types of fields:
   a. Alphanumeric
   b. Numeric
   c. Currency
   d. Date
   e. Memo

2. If you specify the maximum width available for each field, you would not have to plan field widths so carefully. Why is this not done?

3. Why would you not be able to sort names based on last names if you entered both first and last names in one field?

4. Explain what a database structure is and how you make a printout of it.

5. How is a database restructured and why is this done?

6. In what order do you enter records? Why?

7. Describe the process you follow to delete records from a database.

8. How do you "undelete" a record?

9. Sometimes it is impossible to "undelete" records. What causes this to happen and what must you do to correct the problem?

# PROJECTS

## PROJECT 1

### CREATING THE TITLES DATABASE

1. Create a database file named TITLES.
2. Define the fields using the descriptions in the table "The TITLES Database Fields."
3. Print out the file's structure and compare it with the description of the fields in the table.
4. Enter the two records shown in the table "The TITLES Database Records."

### THE TITLES DATABASE FIELDS

| Field | Type/Width |
|---|---|
| ISBN | A5 |
| Title | A18 |
| Author | A7 |
| Edition | A1 |
| Ver | A1 |
| List | $ |

### THE TITLES DATABASE RECORDS

| Field | Record 1 | Record 2 |
|---|---|---|
| ISBN | 96109 | 96110 |
| Title | American History | Working w/ Windows |
| Author | Smith | Henry |
| Edition | 1 | 1 |
| Version | P | P |
| List | 19.95 | 24.95 |

5. Modify the database by adding a new field following the existing *List* field. Name it *Category* and define its type as Memo and its width as 12.
6. Add records to the file from the TITLHOLD file.
7. Fill in the *Category* field for the first two records with **Humanities** (for ISBN 96109) and **Computer Sci** (for ISBN 96110).
8. Print a list of all records in the file.

When you print the TITLES file, your printout should look like this.

```
3/15/93                    Standard Report                      Page 1


ISBN   Title                Author   Edition   Ver  List            Category
-----  -------------------  -------  --------  ---  --------------  ------------
96100  American History     Smith    1         P           19.95 Humanities
96101  Working W/ Windows   Henry    1         P           24.95 Computer Sci
96100  American History     Smith    1         P           19.95 Humanities
96101  Computer Basics      William  1         P           24.95 Computer Sci
96102  Biology Concepts     Franks   3         H           31.95 Science
96103  English Literature   Lewis    1         H           14.95 Humanities
96104  Basic Algebra        O'Neil   1         P           21.95 Math
96105  Basic Physics        Alverez  3         P           29.95 Science
96106  Chemistry            Chin     1         H           31.95 Science
96107  History of Art       Baker    1         P           35.00 Humanities
96108  Basic Programming    Barnes   2         H           26.95 Computer Sci
```

## PROJECT 2

### CREATING THE SALES DATABASE

1. Create a database file named SALES.

## THE SALES DATABASE FIELDS

| Field | Type/Width |
|-------|-----------|
| ISBN | A13 |
| Trade | N |
| Educ | N |
| Mail | N |
| Intntl | N |

2. Define the fields using the descriptions in the table "The SALES Database Fields."

3. Print out the file's structure and compare it with the description of the fields in the table.

4. Enter the two records shown in the table "The SALES Database Records."

## THE SALES DATABASE RECORDS

| Field | Record 1 | Record 2 |
|-------|----------|----------|
| ISBN | 96109 | 96110 |
| Trade | 400 | 300 |
| Educ | 1200 | 900 |
| Mail | 200 | 400 |
| Intntl | 100 | 75 |

5. Modify the database by adding a new field between the existing *ISBN* and *Trade* fields. Name it *Period* and define its type as Alphanumeric and its width as 6.

6. Add records to the file from the SALEHOLD file.

7. Fill in the *Period* field for the first two records with **spring** (for ISBN 96109 and 96110).

8. Print a list of all records in the file.

**When you print the SALES file, your printout should look like this.**

```
3/15/93                      Standard Report                      Page  1


ISBN           Period   Trade   Educ    Mail    Intntl
-----------    ------   ------  ------  ------  ------
96100          Spring    400    1200     200     100
96101          Spring    300     900     400      75
96100          Spring    400    1200     200     100
96101          Spring    300     900     400      75
96102          Spring   1500     300      25    1300
96103          Spring    600     200     100      50
96104          Spring   4000    1000    3000     500
96105          Spring   6000    3000    8000    1200
96106          Spring   3000     750     925     225
96107          Spring     75      25      10       0
96108          Spring    100    2000     156    2000
96100          Fall      300    1100     150      75
96101          Fall      200     800     500     125
96102          Fall     1300     200      75     600
96103          Fall      800     100      75      25
96104          Fall     4000     900    2500     250
96105          Fall     5000    2000    6000       0
96106          Fall     2500     500     625     160
96107          Fall        0      10       5       0
96108          Fall      375    1100     100      50
```

# *Using the Data in a Database*

## *Displaying the Data in a Database*

**After completing this topic, you will be able to:**
- Specify the fields to be displayed using the ASK command
- Use the ASK command to display only certain types of records
- Use the ASK command to display all records except for a certain type
- Use the ASK command to display specified records in reverse order
- Use the ASK command to find records when you are not sure of the record's exact contents
- Print the records displayed by an ASK command

At any point, you can display the data that you have entered into a database with the ASK command. You can tell Paradox to display all of the fields in a record or to display only specific fields. You can also tell Paradox to display (or not display) any duplicate records in the database, or even to display the records in reverse order. In addition, Paradox helps you locate information even if you do not know the exact contents of the records.

Once Paradox locates (and displays) the requested records, you can insert new records, edit existing records or, if necessary, remove records from the database using the standard editing commands.

## ►PARADOX TUTORIAL

In this tutorial, you will use the ASK command to explore a Paradox database table.

### GETTING STARTED

1. If necessary, set the default drive to drive A (or B).
2. Choose ASK from the menu bar and press [Enter←] (or click OK). When the list of files appears, select CUSTOMER. The Query Customer window opens.
3. Make sure that the cursor is in the first field of the Query window, then press [F6]. A check mark appears in all of the other fields.
4. Press [F2] (DO_IT!). An Answer table appears. This table lists all of the unduplicated records in the CUSTOMER file. In other words,

if two of the records in CUSTOMER are identical, only one of them is displayed.

5. Press F8 or click on the little box in the upper-left corner of the window. The Answer table closes.

6. Make sure that the cursor is in the first field of the Query window, then press F6. All the check marks disappear.

### DISPLAYING ONLY SPECIFIC FIELDS

7. Use the arrow keys to move the cursor to the *Id #* field and press F6. A check mark appears. Repeat this procedure in the *Last name*, *First name*, and the *ST* fields.

8. Press F2 (DO_IT!). A new Answer table appears. This time only the *Id #*, *First name*, *Last name*, and *ST* fields are displayed.

### PRINTING THE RESULTS OF A SEARCH

9. Choose REPORT from the menu bar. When the pull-down menu appears, select Output. Press Enter← (or click OK). A list of tables appears.

10. Select the table named ANSWER and press Enter← (or click OK).

11. Select Standard Report from the next dialog box, then choose Printer to print the contents of the Answer table.

12. Press F8 or click on the little box in the upper-left corner of the window. The Answer table closes.

**Using the ASK Command to Display Specific Fields**
If you place a check mark in the *Id #, Last name, First name*, and *ST* fields, this is displayed.

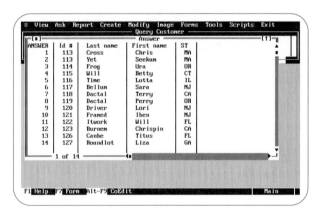

### DISPLAYING ONLY CERTAIN TYPES OF RECORDS

13. Use the arrow keys to move the cursor to the *ST* field. Type **MA** next to the check mark. Make sure that you type **MA** (uppercase) rather than **ma** or **Ma**. Paradox displays only fields that are exact matches for the text that you specify.

14. Press F2 (DO_IT!). A new Answer table appears. Once again, only the *Id #*, *First name*, *Last name*, and *ST* fields are displayed, but in addition, *only records with MA in the ST field are displayed.*

15. Press F8 or click on the little box in the upper-left corner of the window. The Answer table closes.

16. Use ←Bksp to erase *MA* in the *ST* field. Type **CA** in the same location. Remember to use all uppercase letters or your answer table will be empty.

17. Press [F2] (DO_IT!). A new Answer table appears. Once again, only the *Id #*, *First name*, *Last name*, and *ST* fields are displayed, but this time, only records with *CA* in the *ST* field are displayed.
18. Press [F8] or click on the little box in the upper-left corner of the window. The Answer table closes.

**Using ASK to Display Certain Types of Records**
When you type **CA** in the *ST* field (next to the check mark), this is what you will see.

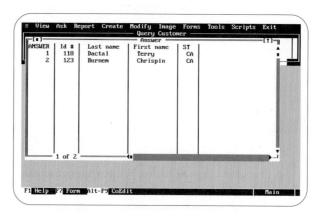

## DISPLAYING MORE THAN ONE TYPE OF RECORD

19. Use the arrow keys to move the cursor to the *ST* field (if it is not already there). Change the entry in the *ST* field so that it reads **CA or MA**. Remember that *CA* and *MA* must be in uppercase, but you can type the word *or* in upper- or lowercase—Paradox doesn't care. Also, you must separate each part of the entry with a space. In other words, type **CA**(space)**or**(space)**MA**.
20. Press [F2] (DO_IT!). A new Answer table appears. Only the *Id #*, *First name*, *Last name*, and *ST* fields are displayed, but this time, all records with *CA* **and** *MA* in the *ST* field are displayed.
21. Press [F8] or click on the little box in the upper-left corner of the window. The Answer table closes.

## LEAVING SPECIFIC RECORDS OUT OF THE LISTING

22. Use the arrow keys to move the cursor to the *ST* field (if it is not already there). Change the entry in the *ST* field so that it reads **not CA**. Remember that *CA* must be in uppercase, and you must type a space after the word *not*.
23. Press [F2] (DO_IT!). A new Answer table appears. Again, only the *Id #*, *First name*, *Last name*, and *ST* fields are displayed, but only the records that *do not* have *CA* in the *ST* field are displayed.
24. Press [F8] or click on the little box in the upper-left corner of the window. The Answer table closes.

## DISPLAYING THE RECORDS IN REVERSE ORDER

25. Use the arrow keys to move the cursor to the *ST* field (if it is not already there). Use [← Bksp] to clear the entry that is there.
26. Move the cursor to the *Id #* field and press [F6]. The check mark displayed there disappears. Press [Ctrl]-[F6]. A check mark next to a down arrow symbol appears.
27. Press [F2] (DO_IT!). Only the *Id #*, *First name*, *Last name*, and *ST* fields are displayed,  but this time, they are displayed in reverse

order based on the *Id #* field. In other words, the largest Id number is at the top of the list, and the smallest is at the bottom.

28. Press F8 or click on the little box in the upper-left corner of the window. The Answer table closes.

**Using ASK to Display Records in Reverse Order**
If you mark the first field using Ctrl-F6, the selected records display in reverse order based on the first field.

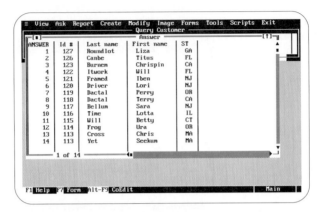

## DISPLAYING ALL RECORDS—EVEN IF THEY ARE DUPLICATED

29. Use the arrow keys to move the cursor to the *Id #* field (if it is not already there). Press Ctrl-F6 to clear the field.

30. With the cursor still in the *Id #* field, press Alt-F6. A check mark next to a plus sign (+) appears.

31. Press F2 (DO_IT!). Again, only the *Id #*, *First name*, *Last name*, and *ST* fields are displayed, but this time, all records in the database are displayed, *even if some of the records are exact duplicates*.

32. Press F8 or click on the little box in the upper-left corner of the window. The Answer table closes.

## DISPLAYING RECORDS EVEN IF YOU ARE NOT SURE OF THE EXACT CONTENTS

33. Use the arrow keys to move the cursor to the *Id #* field (if it is not already there). Press Alt-F6 to clear the field.

34. With the cursor still in the *Id #* field, press F6. A check mark appears.

35. Use the arrow keys to move the cursor to the *Last name* field. Type **like dac** next to the check mark.

36. Press F2 (DO_IT!). Again, only the *Id #*, *First name*, *Last name*, and *ST* fields are displayed, and all records that contain an entry *similar* to *dac* in the *Last name* field are displayed.

**Displaying Records When You Are Not Sure of the Exact Contents**
You can use the LIKE operator to display all records that are similar to the information specified during a query operation.

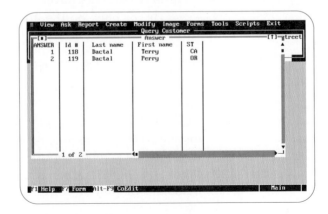

37. Press F8 or click on the little box in the upper-left corner of the window. The Answer table closes.

38. Use ← Bksp to clear the entry in the *Last name* field, then type **d..** (including the two periods) next to the check mark.

39. Press F2 (DO_IT!). Only the *Id #, First name, Last name,* and *ST* fields are displayed, and all records that begin with the letter *d* are displayed.

**FINISHING UP**

40. You have completed this tutorial. Press Alt - F8 to close all files that are open. Go on to the next activity or exit the program.

► **QUICK REFERENCE**

The ASK command is used to examine all or any part of a Paradox database table.

## Displaying All Fields
To display the records in a file, choose ASK from the menu bar. When the Query window appears, move the cursor to the first field (if it is not already there), and press F6. A check mark appears in all of the other fields. Press F2 (DO_IT!) to see a list of your records.

## Displaying Selected Fields
When you are only interested in the data in specific fields, move the cursor in the Query window to the fields that you want to display and make sure that a check mark is displayed in each one. Clear the check mark from any fields that you do not want to examine.

## Displaying Selected Fields with Specific Contents
When you are only interested in the records that contain a certain type of data, move the cursor (in the Query window) to the correct field, make sure that a check mark is displayed, and specify the type of data that you want to see.

## Displaying Records When You Are Not Sure of the Exact Contents
When you need to examine the contents of a group of records but cannot remember the exact contents of those records, you can use the LIKE operator or wildcards to help Paradox locate the information you need.

The LIKE operator is used in a field along with an entry that is similar to the data needed. For example, if you enter **LIKE SMITH**, Paradox locates any record that contains any entry that is similar, such as *SMYTH, SMYTHE,* or even *SIMTHE.*

Paradox also accepts two wildcard characters. Two periods (..) can represent any number of characters and one (or more) "@" signs can each represent a single character. For example, if you type **R..E**, Paradox locates all records that begin with the letter *R*, end with the letter *E*, and have any number of characters in between. However, if you type **R@@E**, Paradox displays only information that begins with *R*, ends with *E*, and has only two characters in between.

► E X E R C I S E S

## EXERCISE 1

### DISPLAYING SELECTED FIELDS IN THE EMPLOYEE FILE

1. If necessary, set the default drive to drive A (or B).
2. Choose ASK from the menu bar. When the file list displays, select the EMPLOYEE database.
3. Use the arrow keys to move the cursor to and place a check mark in the *Employee #*, *Last name*, *First name*, and *Payrate* fields. In other words, move to each of these fields and press F6.
4. Press F2 (DO_IT!) to display the selected fields and records.
5. Print a list of the records.
6. Close all files.

**Displaying Selected Fields in the EMPLOYEE File**
Your printout for Exercise 1 should look like the information shown here.

```
 2/16/93            Standard Report          Page    1


 Employee #   Last Name    First Name   Payrate
 ----------   ----------   ----------   ----------------
    101       Saucer       Coopen              7.50
    102       Schwartz     Bermuda             7.00
    105       Minute       Ina                 8.50
    106       Will         Betty               7.00
    107       Beef         Sida                8.00
    108       Dune         Lorna               6.50
    109       Earl         Duka                8.00
    110       Binone       Ida                 6.75
    111       Rose         Lieca               8.50
    112       DeVille      Marguerite          7.50
    113       Minute       Justa               7.00
```

## EXERCISE 2

### DISPLAYING SELECTED FIELDS IN THE TIME FILE

1. Open the ASK menu and select the TIME file.
2. Select the *Employee #* and *Hours* fields. Press F2 (DO_IT!) to display the selected fields and records.
3. Print a list of the records.
4. Close all files.

**Displaying Selected Fields in the TIME File**
Your printout for Exercise 2 should look like the information shown here.

```
 2/16/93            Standard Report          Page    1

 Employee #   Hours
 ----------   ----------------
    105              20.00
    105              25.00
    106              20.00
    106              37.00
    107              10.00
    107              40.00
    108              25.00
    108              40.00
    109              40.00
    110              30.00
    110              40.00
    111              20.00
    111              40.00
    112              40.00
    113              40.00
```

# Using Relational Operators to Filter Records

**After completing this topic, you will be able to:**

■ Use relational operators, such as greater than (>) and equal to (=), so that only those records that match the condition are displayed

In previous topics, you have used several commands that display records for editing or deletion. When your database is small, finding a specific record is not difficult, but as your database gets larger, it becomes harder to find the records that you want. Database management programs like Paradox help you find one or more records by using relational operators that "filter" the records that are displayed. In other words, only those records that match the specified criteria are displayed.

For example, to answer a question such as "What customers have a balance due greater than $25?" you would specify a condition in the *Amount* field that reads *>25*. This command displays only those records of customers whose amount is greater than $25.

Keep in mind that Paradox is case sensitive, so if you refer to the state *MA*, don't enter it as **ma** or **Ma** in your commands.

## ▶ PARADOX® TUTORIAL

In this tutorial, you will use relational operators to filter records in the CUSTOMER database file.

### GETTING STARTED

1. If necessary, set the default drive to drive A (or B).

### FILTERING RECORDS WITH RELATIONAL OPERATORS

2. Choose ASK from the menu bar, and press Enter←⏎. When the list of tables appears, choose CUSTOMER.
3. Select the *Last name*, *First name*, *ST*, *Area*, *Date*, and *Age* fields by moving the cursor to each field and pressing F6.
4. Move the cursor to the *Age* field and type **>50** next to the check mark. Press F2 (DO-IT!) to list only records with ages over, but not equal to, 50.
5. When you are finished examining the records that were found, press F8 to close the Answer table.

6. Erase >50 from the *Age* field, move the cursor to the *Area* field, and type **=201** next to the check mark. Press F2 (DO-IT!) to list only the records with *201* in the *Area* field.

7. Press F8 to close the Answer table.

8. Erase *=201* from the *Area* field, move the cursor to the *ST* field, and type **=MA** next to the check mark. Press F2 (DO-IT!) to list only the records with *MA* in the *ST* field.

9. Press F8 to close the Answer table.

10. Erase *=MA* from the *ST* field, move the cursor to the *Date* field, and type **>12/30/92** next to the check mark. Press F2 (DO-IT!) to list only the records with dates later than 12/30/92.

11. Choose REPORT from the menu bar and print the contents of this Answer table.

12. Press Alt-F8 to close all open files and clear the Paradox desktop.

**Filtering Records with Relational Operators**
This is what your printout should look like after you filter the CUSTOMER database.

```
2/16/93          Standard Report          Page    1


Last name    First name   ST   Area  Date       Age
----------   ----------   --   ----  --------   ------
Burnem       Chrispin     CA   415   2/12/93       27
Canbe        Titus        FL   415   3/12/93       35
Itwork       Will         FL   407   1/10/93       26
Roundlot     Liza         GA   404   3/05/93       89
```

## DISPLAYING SELECTED FIELDS IN FILTERED RECORDS

13. Choose ASK from the menu bar, and press Enter↵. When the list of tables appears, choose CUSTOMER.

14. Select the *Last name*, *First name*, and *Date* fields by moving the cursor to each field and pressing F6.

15. Move the cursor to the *ST* field and type **=MA**. Notice that because there is no check mark in the *ST* field, it will not display in the Answer table. Press F2 (DO-IT!) to list only the *Last name*, *First Name*, and *Date* fields for records with *MA* in the *ST* field.

16. Press F8 to close the Answer table.

17. Use ←Bksp to erase *=MA* from the *ST* field.

18. Move the cursor to the *Age* field and type **>=40**. Press F2 (DO-IT!) to list only the *Last name*, *First name*, and *Date* fields for records with ages greater than or equal to 40.

## CONTINUING ON YOUR OWN

19. The Quick Reference section in this topic describes relational operators. You might want to experiment more with these before proceeding. If you make any mistakes, the program will respond with an error message. To try again, press Alt-F8 and start over.

## FINISHING UP

20. You have completed this tutorial. Press Alt-F8 to close all open files and clear the Paradox desktop. Go on to the next activity or exit the program.

Relational operators are used to compare the data in a field to a number, character string, date, or logical statement to determine their relationship. For example, relational operators can determine if one field's value is larger or smaller than another, has an earlier or later date, or comes before or after it alphabetically.

## Greater Than

The greater-than operator (>) finds all records greater than, but not equal to, the criteria you specify. For example:

- **>Jones** displays all records alphabetically after *Jones*, but does not include *Jones*.
- **>10.00** finds all records where the amount is more than, but not equal to, 10.00.
- **>1/10/93** finds all records where the date is later than January 10, 1993. January 10, 1993 is not included.

## Less Than

The less-than operator (<) finds all records less than, but not equal to, the criteria you specify. For example:

- **<Jones** displays all records alphabetically before *Jones*, but does not include *Jones*.
- **<10.00** finds all records where the amount is less than, but not equal to, 10.00.
- **<1/10/93** finds all records where the date is earlier than January 10, 1993. January 10, 1993 is not included.

## Equal To

The equal-to operator (=) finds all records exactly equal to the criteria you specify. For example:

- **=Jones** finds all records with *Jones* as a last name.
- **=10.00** finds all records where the amount is exactly 10.00.
- **=1/10/93** finds all records dated January 10, 1993.

## Greater Than or Equal To

The greater-than-or-equal-to operator (>=) finds all records greater than or equal to the criteria you specify. For example:

- **>=Jones** finds all records with *Jones* as a last name, and all last names that follow *Jones* alphabetically.
- **>=10.00** finds all records where the amount is 10.00 or more.
- **>=1/10/93** finds all records where the date is January 10, 1993 or later.

## Less Than or Equal To

The less-than-or-equal-to operator (<=) finds all records less than or equal to the criteria you specify. For example:

- **<=Jones** finds all records with *Jones* as a last name, and all last names that precede *Jones* alphabetically.
- **<=10.00** finds all records where the amount is 10.00 or less.

■ **<=1/10/93** finds all records where the date is January 10, 1993 or earlier.

### Not Equal To

The not-equal-to keyword (*not*) finds all records not exactly equal to the criteria you specify. For example:

■ **not Jones** displays all records *except* those with *Jones* as a last name.
■ **not 10.00** finds all records where the amount is not anything *but* 10.00.
■ **not 1/10/93** finds all records *not* dated January 10, 1993.

## ► EXERCISES

### EXERCISE 1

### FILTERING RECORDS IN THE EMPLOYEE FILE

1. If necessary, set the default drive to A (or B).
2. Choose ASK from the menu bar and select EMPLOYEE from the list of tables.
3. Use the arrow keys and F6 to place a check mark in the *Employee #*, *Last name*, *First name*, *City*, *Department*, and *Payrate* fields.
4. Print a list of only those records that have *1* in the *Department* field.
5. Print a list of only those records that have *Largo* in the *City* field.
6. Print a list of only those records that have *less* than $7.00 in the *Payrate* field.

### EXERCISE 2

### FILTERING RECORDS IN THE TIME FILE

1. Choose ASK from the menu bar and select TIME from the list of tables. Move the cursor to the first column (TIME) and press F6. A check mark should appear in all of the other fields.
2. Print a list of only those records that have *2* in the *Shift* field.
3. Print a list of only those records that have *less* than 40 hours in the *Hours* field.
4. Print a list of only those records that have employee numbers *higher* than 110.

# *Using Logical Operators to Filter Records*

**After completing this topic, you will be able to:**

- Enter the logical operators AND and OR to select specific records
- Enter the logical operator NOT to display records that do not meet the specified criteria
- Replace the field contents of selected records with the CHANGETO command and Example Elements
- Locate records or groups of records using the FIND operator
- Remove  specified records from your database with the DELETE operator
- Use Example Elements to change data in numeric fields

On occasion, you will need to use two or more criteria to locate the data that you need. For example, if you need to know how much money customer 101 spent on 12/10/92, you would ask Paradox to display all records that contain the number *101* in the *Customer Number* field **and** *12/10/92* in the *Date* field.

In another situation, you may need to examine the data for anyone that lives in CA *or* anyone that lives in MA. In this case, if you don't want to make a separate list for each state, you can instruct Paradox to list all records that meet either condition.

Similarly, if you need to see the data for everyone *except* for the people that spent more than $100.00, you can tell Paradox *not* to display the records that have a value greater than 100 in the *Price* field.

## P A R A D O X   T U T O R I A L

In this tutorial, you will use logical operators to examine records in the CUSTOMER database file. You will then apply this procedure to replace data in selected fields and locate records with specific contents.

### GETTING STARTED

1. If necessary, set the default drive to A (or B).

### USING THE OR OPERATOR

2. Choose ASK from the menu bar and press (Enter ←⏎). When the list of tables appears, choose CUSTOMER.
3. Select the *Id #*, *Last name*, *First name*, *ST*, *Date*, and *Age* fields by moving the cursor to each field and pressing ( F6 ).

4. Move the cursor to the *ST* field and type **MA or NJ**. Press F2 (DO-IT!) to display only records with *MA* or *NJ* in the *ST* field. When you finish, press F8 to close the Answer table. Then use ←Bksp to erase the entry in the *ST* field.

5. Move the cursor to the *Age* field and type **>60 or <5**. Press F2 (DO-IT!) to display only records with ages greater than 60 *or* less than 5. When you finish, press F8 to close the Answer table. Then use ←Bksp to erase the entry in the *Age* field.

6. Press the down arrow to create a second line in the Query window. Move the cursor to each field on this line and press F6 again to place a second check mark in the *Id #*, *Last name*, *First name*, *ST*, *Date*, and *Age* fields.

7. Type **>1/05/93** in the *Date* field on the *first* line and **>40** in the *Age* field on the *second* line. Press F2 (DO-IT!) to display only the records for customers who made a purchase after January 5, 1993 *or* who are more than 40 years old.

8. Press Alt-F8 to close all windows and clear the desktop.

## USING THE AND OPERATOR

9. Choose ASK from the menu bar. When the list of tables appears, choose CUSTOMER.

10. Select the *Id #*, *Last name*, *First name*, *ST*, *Date*, and *Age* fields by moving the cursor to each field and pressing F6.

11. Move the cursor to the *Date* field and·type **>1/05/93.** Move the cursor to the *Age* field and type **>40**. Press F2 (DO-IT!) to display only records for customers who made a purchase after 1/5/93 *and* who are more than 40 years old.

12. Press F8 to close the Answer table, use ←Bksp to erase the entries in the *Date* and *Age* fields, then move the cursor to the *ST* field and type **CA.** Next, move the cursor to the *Id #* field and type **>118**. Press F2 (DO-IT!) to display only records with *CA* in the *ST* field *and* Id numbers higher than 118.

## COMPARING RESULTS

13. Choose REPORT from the menu bar and print the list of records found in Step 12.

14. Press F8 to close the Answer table. Press the down arrow to create a second line in the Query window. Press F6 to place a second check mark (on the second line) in the *Id #*, *Last name*, *First name*, *ST*, *Date*, and *Age* fields.

15. Move to the *ST* field and use ←Bksp to clear the entry on the first line. Press the down arrow and type **CA** in the *ST* field on the *second* line. Press F2 (Do-It!). All records that have *CA* in the *ST* field *or* have an Id number greater than 118 are displayed.

16. Choose REPORT from the menu bar, print the new list of records, and compare this list to the printout from Step 13.

### NOTE

You must enter different OR conditions for different fields on separate lines. All of the lines must have the same fields checked or the query will not work. You can enter up to 64 lines on a single query.

**Comparing the AND and OR Operations**

The AND operation displays records that have the specified data in both the *ST* and *Id #* fields. The OR operation displays all records that meet either criteria.

```
2/16/93            Standard Report            Page    1



Id #   Last name     First name   ST   Date        Age
----   ----------    ----------   --   --------    ------
123    Burnem        Chrispin     CA   2/12/93       27
```

```
2/16/93            Standard Report            Page    1


Id #   Last name     First name   ST   Date        Age
----   ----------    ----------   --   --------    ------
118    Dactal        Terry        CA   8/01/92        3
119    Dactal        Perry        OR   6/03/92       22
120    Driver        Lori         NJ   9/06/92       39
121    Framed        Iben         NJ   10/15/92      25
122    Itwork        Will         FL   1/10/93       26
123    Burnem        Chrispin     CA   2/12/93       27
126    Canbe         Titus        FL   3/12/93       35
127    Roundlot      Liza         GA   3/05/93       89
```

17. Close the Answer table and use ⟨← Bksp⟩ to clear all entries from both lines in the Query window.

18. Move the cursor to the *Date* field on the first line and type **>01/01/93.** Press the down arrow, move to the *Age* field, and type **>30** on the second line. Press ⟨F2⟩ (DO-IT!) to display only records that have either the specified date *or* age.

19. Choose REPORT from the menu bar and print the list of records found.

20. Close the Answer table and use ⟨← Bksp⟩ to erase the entry from the *Age* field on the second line of the Query window.

21. Use the arrow keys to move to each field on the second line of the Query window. Press ⟨F6⟩ to clear each field. In other words, when you finish this step, all of the check marks on the second line should be gone.

22. Move to the *Age* field (on the first line) and type **>30.** Press ⟨F2⟩ (DO-IT!) to display only records that have both the specified date *and* age.

23. Choose REPORT from the menu bar, print the new list of records, and compare this list to the previous printout.

**More Comparisons of the AND and OR Operations**

The operation using OR displays records that have the specified data in either the *Date* or *Age* fields. The AND operation displays only those records that meet both criteria.

```
2/16/93            Standard Report            Page    1

Id #   Last name     First name   ST   Date        Age
----   ----------    ----------   --   --------    ------
113    Yet           Seekum       MA   1/07/92       63
114    Frog          Ura          OR   1/10/92       45
115    Will          Betty        CT   1/16/92       33
117    Bellum        Sara         NJ   3/06/92       34
120    Driver        Lori         NJ   9/06/92       39
122    Itwork        Will         FL   1/10/93       26
123    Burnem        Chrispin     CA   2/12/93       27
126    Canbe         Titus        FL   3/12/93       35
127    Roundlot      Liza         GA   3/05/93       89
```

```
2/16/93            Standard Report            Page    1

Id #   Last name     First name   ST   Date        Age
----   ----------    ----------   --   --------    ------
126    Canbe         Titus        FL   3/12/93       35
127    Roundlot      Liza         GA   3/05/93       89
```

24. Press ⟨Alt⟩-⟨F8⟩ to close all windows and clear the desktop.

## USING THE NOT OPERATOR

25. Choose ASK from the menu bar and press [Enter ←]. When the list of tables appears, choose CUSTOMER.

26. Select the *Id #*, *Last name*, *First name*, *ST*, *Date*, and *Age* fields by moving the cursor to each field and pressing [F6].

27. Move to the *Age* field and type **not >30**. Press [F2] to display only records with ages *not greater* than 30.

28. Close the Answer table and use [← Bksp] to erase the entry in the *Age* field. Move to the *ST* field, type **not =CA**, and press [F2] to display only records *without CA* in the *ST* field.

29. Press [Alt]-[F8] to clear the desktop and close all windows.

30. Choose ASK from the menu bar and press [Enter ←]. When the list of tables appears, choose PURCHASE.

31. Move to the first field (PURCHASE) and press [F6] to place a check mark in every field.

32. Move to the *Payment Method* field and type **Cash**. Press [F2] to display all purchases in the table that were paid in cash.

    Hint: When you type the word *Cash*, be sure to enter upper and lowercase letters as shown.

33. Close the Answer table, move to the *Payment Method* field, and change the entry to read **not Cash**. Press [F2] to display all purchases in the table that were *not* paid in cash.

34. Close the Answer table, move to the *Amount* field, type **>15**, and press [F2]. This displays only records with an amount larger than 15, which was not paid in cash. Print a list of the records.

**The NOT Operation**
In this example, only records with an amount greater than 15, which was NOT paid in cash, are displayed.

| 2/16/93 | | Standard Report | | Page 1 |
|---|---|---|---|---|
| ID# | Date | Item Description | Amount | Payment Method |
| --- | -------- | -------------------------- | ----------------- | -------------- |
| 118 | 11/16/93 | Flamingo Croquet Set | 57.77 | Charg |
| 121 | 7/10/94 | Top Hat (size 6-7/8) | 59.75 | Charg |
| 123 | 4/19/92 | Chess Board | 39.95 | Check |
| 123 | 3/17/93 | White Rabbit (back order) | 29.95 | Charg |

35. Press [Alt]-[F8] to clear the desktop and close all windows.

## REPLACING DATA IN SELECTED FIELDS

To change data in selected fields you need to use the CHANGETO operator. For example, if you type **Rabbit, changeto Bird** in the *Product* field, Paradox locates all records that have the entry *Rabbit* in the specified field, and changes that entry to *Bird*.

**NOTE**

You must type a comma to separate the field contents from the CHANGETO operator or the command will not work.

36. Choose ASK from the menu bar and press [Enter ←]. When the list of tables appears, choose PURCHASE.

37. Move to the *Item Description* field, and type **Calico Cat, changeto Cheshire Cat (incomplete)**. Press [F2] (DO-IT!). A window opens that displays records that were changed.

    Hint: Be sure to type a comma after **Calico Cat**.

38. When you are finished, press [Alt]-[F8] to clear the desktop.

39. Open the VIEW menu. When the list of files appears, choose PURCHASE. When the View window opens, you will see that all of the records that read *Calico Cat* now say *Cheshire Cat*.

40. Choose REPORT from the menu bar and print this list. When you are finished, press [Alt]-[F8] to clear the desktop.

## CHANGING NUMERIC DATA IN SELECTED FIELDS

To change numeric data in specified fields, you must use what is called an *Example Element*. Paradox uses Example Elements as place holders while it performs calculations.

To create an Example Element, make up a short name, press [F5], and type that name in the correct part of the formula. As you type, the Example Element displays in reverse type (also called reverse video) on your screen.

In the following exercise, you will use *AMT1* as an Example Element, but you could use any name that you want as long as it does not contain any spaces or other punctuation. In other words, an Example Element can contain numbers and letters in any combination.

41. Choose ASK from the menu bar. When the list of tables appears, choose PURCHASE.

42. Move to the *Amount* field, type **>0, AMT1, changeto AMT1 + .50**, and press [F2] (DO-IT!).

43. A window opens that lists all of the records that were changed. Choose REPORT from the menu bar, then Output. When the list appears, choose CHANGED and print the table.

44. Open the REPORT menu again. When the list appears, choose PURCHASE, and print the table. Compare your new printout to the printout from Step 43. You will see that all of the values in the *Amount* field have increased by .50. When you are finished, press [Alt]-[F8] to clear the desktop.

45. Choose ASK from the menu bar. When the list of tables appears, choose PURCHASE. Move to the *Amount* field, type **>0, AMT1, changeto AMT1 - .50**, and press [F2] (DO-IT!). All of the changed records return to their original values.

46. When you are finished, press [Alt]-[F8] to close all windows and clear the desktop.

## USING THE FIND COMMAND

47. Choose ASK from the menu bar and press [Enter ←]. When the list of tables appears, choose CUSTOMER.

48. Move the cursor to the first column (CUSTOMER) and type **FIND**.

49. Move the cursor to the *ST* field and type **CA**. Press [F2] (DO-IT!). A window opens that displays the entire CUSTOMER database, but the cursor will be on the first record that displays *CA* in the *ST* field.

50. Open the VIEW menu. When the list appears, choose ANSWER. This window displays all of the records in the database with *CA* in the *ST* field.

## FINISHING UP

51. You have completed this tutorial. Press [Alt]-[F8] to clear the desktop and close all open files. Go to the next activity or exit the program.

> **HINT**
>
> Be sure to include the commas and remember to press [F5] each time before you type the name of the Example Element, **AMT1**.

Use logical operators to connect two or more criteria. For example, they can specify that only records meeting two or more criteria are displayed.

### AND Operations

When you specify an AND operation, every condition must be met. For example, if you type **=10.00** in the *Amount* field and **=Jones** in the *Last name* field, Paradox finds all records where the amount is 10.00 *and* the last name is Jones.

### OR Operations

When you specify an OR operation, at least one condition must be met; however, all conditions can also be met. For example, if you type **MA or NJ** in the *ST* field, The program finds all records where the *ST* field contains MA *or* NJ.

If you need to locate records with an amount of 10.00 *or* a last name of Jones, you need to use two lines in a Query window. Type the first criteria on the first line, press the down arrow to create a second line, and type the second criteria there. In other words, different criteria for different fields must appear on separate lines.

### NOT Operations

When you specify a NOT operation, the specified condition must not be met. For example, **not 10.00** finds all records where the amount is *not* 10.00.

### Replacing Data in Selected Fields

When you want to make the same change to a number of records, you can update the contents of fields automatically using the CHANGETO operator. For example, if all prices are to increase 5 percent, you don't need to edit each record individually. CHANGETO can update all records automatically.

When you specify **changeto**, Paradox replaces the current contents of a specified field with new contents. For example, the command **TweedleDee, changeto TweedleDum** replaces the existing entry (TweedleDee) with a new entry (TweedleDum). Remember to type a comma after the existing entry (before the CHANGETO operator) or the command will not work.

You can replace the contents of a field in all records just as easily as you can replace the contents of a field in one record. Just type **changeto** followed by the new entry, and press ⌈F2⌉. In other words, if you type **changeto 111** in the *Id #* field, Paradox changes all Id numbers in all records to *111*.

### Using Example Elements

To change data in Numeric fields, you must use an Example Element. Paradox uses Example Elements as place holders while it performs calculations.

To create an Example Element, make up a short name, press ⌈F5⌉, and type that name in the correct part of the formula. As you type, the Example Element displays in reverse type on your screen. An Example Element can contain numbers and letters in any combination.

For example, if you need to increase all prices in a database by 5%, open a Query window, locate the *Price* field, and type **>0, PRICE, changeto PRICE * 1.05**. This command locates all items that have a price greater than 0, temporarily refers to that amount as PRICE, and increases its value by 5%.

Remember to press F5 each time before you type the name of the Example Element, and that it appears in reverse type. Also, be sure to type  commas to separate each part of the command.

In general, to create a numeric CHANGETO statement, specify a criterion, type a comma, press F5, assign a name for the Example Element, type another comma, and enter the formula that defines the change you want to make.

### The FIND Operator

The FIND operator finds the first record that matches a specified condition, displays the entire database, and moves the cursor to that record. For example, type **FIND** in the first column of a Query window, then type **CA** in the *ST* field. Paradox displays the entire database, and the cursor will be on the first record that has *CA* in the *ST* field. You can then press F9 (EDIT) to change this entry if necessary.

# ► E X E R C I S E S

## EXERCISE 1

### FILTERING RECORDS IN THE EMPLOYEE FILE

1. Choose ASK from the menu bar and open the EMPLOYEE file.
2. Use the cursor and F6 to select the *Last name*, *First name*, *City*, *Department*, and *Payrate* fields.
3. Print the records for employees who live in Largo *and* are assigned to department 1.
4. Print the records for employees who live in Largo *or* are assigned to department 1.
5. Print the  records for employees who live in Largo *and* are assigned to department 2.
6. Print the records for employees who live in Largo *or* are assigned to department 2.
7. Print the records for employees who live in Tampa *and* make more than $7.50 per hour.
8. Print the  records  for  employees  who  live  in  Tampa  *and*  make exactly $7.50 per hour.
9. Print the records for employees who live in Tampa *and* make less than $7.50 per hour.
10. Print the records for employees who live in Tampa *and* make $7.50 or more per hour.
11. Print the records for employees who *do not* live in Tampa *and* make $7.00 or more per hour.

12. Print the records for employees who live in Tampa *and* do not make $7.50 or more per hour.

---

## EXERCISE 2

---

### FILTERING RECORDS IN THE TIME FILE

1. Choose ASK from the menu bar and open the TIME file.
2. Print the records for employees who worked 40 hours on shift 3.
3. Print the records for employees who worked 40 hours *or* worked on shift 3.
4. Print the records for employees who did not work *exactly* 40 hours.

---

## EXERCISE 3

---

### REPLACING DATA IN THE EMPLOYEE FILE

1. Choose ASK from the menu bar and open the EMPLOYEE file.
2. Increase all numbers in the *Payrate* field by 5 percent (RATE * 1.05).
3. Print a list of the records that were changed and the updated EMPLOYEE file, but only display the *Employee #*, *Last name*, *First name*, and *Payrate* fields.

*Quiz - Tue*
*Page 51*
*Fill-in*
*use p50 as notes*

*Tree/F >prn*

# Creating & Printing Reports—The Basics

**After completing this topic, you will be able to:**
- Describe the parts of a typical report
- Print an "Instant Report"
- Create a report with the CREATE-REPORT command sequence
- Preview a report before you send it to the printer
- Print a report with the OUTPUT command
- Modify a report by editing the Report Specifications

Most people in a business do not use the actual database that is stored on disks. Generally, they use printed reports created from all or part of the information stored in the database. The full database might contain information about all aspects of the business, but part of the information is needed by the sales manager, other parts are of interest to the company president, and some of the data are needed by the finance department. Rather than print a gigantic report that contains all information for all departments, you design reports to organize specific information in a way that each department can use. In other words, each report provides only the information each person or department needs.

## ▶ P A R A D O X   T U T O R I A L

In this tutorial, you will create a report for the CUSTOMER file that contains only the first name, last name, area code, and telephone number fields from all records. You will then modify the report to add purchase dates.

**GETTING STARTED**

1. If necessary, set the default drive to drive A (or B).

**CREATING A REPORT**

2. Choose REPORT from the menu bar. When the pull-down menu appears, select Design.
3. When the Table Selection window appears, locate the CUSTOMER database file.

**ADDING A HEADING**

**NOTE**

The description you type will appear as a title at the top of the finished report.

4. When the next dialog box appears, choose the first numbered item from the list. It should be labeled *Unused Report*. Type the

description **Phone Numbers** in the box that appears, and press Enter ← (or click OK).

5. When the last selection box appears, choose Tabular, and press Enter ← (or click OK). The Report Design screen appears.

**The Report Design Screen**
You use this screen to design custom reports for your database.

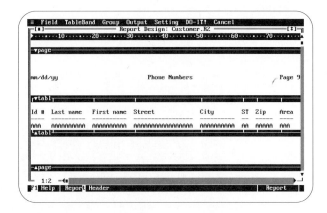

**DEFINING THE COLUMNS**

6. Use the arrow keys to move the cursor to the *Id #* field, then choose TABLEBAND from the menu bar. When the pull-down menu appears, select Erase. Press Enter ←, and the *Id #* field disappears.

7. Move the cursor to the *Street* field, and choose TABLEBAND again. When the pull-down menu appears, select Erase a second time. Press Enter ←, and the *Street* field disappears.

**NOTE**

If you make a mistake during this procedure, choose CANCEL from the menu bar and start over.

8. Repeat Step 7, but this time move the cursor to the *City* field.

9. Repeat Step 7, but this time move the cursor to the *ST* field.

10. Repeat Step 7, but this time move the cursor to the *Zip* field.

11. Repeat Step 7, but this time move the cursor to the *Date* field.

12. Repeat Step 7, but this time move the cursor to the *Age* field.

13. Repeat Step 7, but this time move the cursor to the *Remarks* field. When you have finished this step, only the *Last name*, *First name*, *Area*, and *Phone* fields should display.

14. Use the arrow keys to place the cursor at the end of the text for the Last name column. In other words, move it to the space after the end of the words *Last name* as shown in the illustration.

**Designing a Custom Report**
Be sure that the cursor is in this location before you perform Step 15.

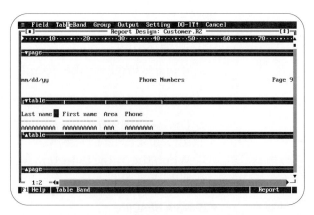

15. Choose TABLEBAND from the menu bar. When the pull-down menu appears, choose Resize, and press Enter ←. Press the right

arrow key three times to make the *First name* field three characters larger, then press Enter⏎ again.

16. Repeat Step 15 in the *First name* field.
17. Repeat Step 15 in the *Area* field.
18. Repeat Step 15 in the *Phone* field, but in this column press the right arrow key *five* times.
19. Use the arrow keys (or the mouse) to move the cursor to the text that reads *Phone* at the top of the Phone column. Press Del five times to erase this block of text.
20. Use the arrow keys or the mouse to move the cursor to the text that reads *Area* at the top of the Area column. Press Del four times to erase this block of text. When it is gone, type **Phone** at the top of the Area column, as shown in the illustration.
21. Finally, use the arrow keys (or the mouse) to move the cursor to the gap that follows the dashed line below *Phone*, and press the hyphen [ - ]] until this gap is filled in.

**Designing a Custom Report (continued)**
This is how the Report Design screen should look when you finish Step 21.

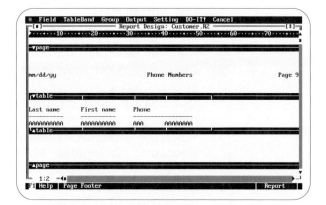

**SAVING THE REPORT FORMAT**

22. Press F2 (DO-IT!). Paradox saves your report format.

**DISPLAYING AND PRINTING THE REPORT**

23. Choose REPORT from the menu bar. When the pull-down menu appears, select Output.
24. Load the CUSTOMER database from the list of files that is displayed.
25. Choose Phone Numbers from the list of reports that is displayed, and press Enter⏎ or click OK.
26. When the next box appears, select Printer. The contents of your database will be printed according to the guidelines defined in the Phone List report form.

**The Completed Phone List Report**
This is how your new custom report will look after it is printed.

```
2/18/93              Phone Numbers          Page    1



Last name         First name      Phone
----------        ----------      ------------------
Itwork            Will            407     555-1265
Burnem            Chrispin        415     555-2653
Canbe             Titus           415     555-2731
Roundalot         Liza            404     555-8764
Will              Betty           203     555-1001
Will              Betty           203     555-1001
Cross             Chris           617     555-1002
Time              Lotta           312     555-1003
Driver            Lori            201     555-1004
Dactal            Terry           408     555-1005
Bellum            Sara            201     555-1006
Yet               Seekum          617     555-1007
Dactal            Perry           508     555-1008
Frog              Ura             508     555-1009
Framed            Iben            201     555-1010
```

## MODIFYING THE REPORT

Remember, if you make a mistake you can always select CANCEL from the menu bar and start over at Step 23.

27. Choose REPORT from the menu bar. When the pull-down menu appears, select Change. Use the Selection window to choose the CUSTOMER database, then choose Phone Numbers from the list of reports that you see.

28. When the Report description box appears, change the text to read: **Customer Phone List - Master**. When you are done, press Enter↵ or click OK. The Report Design screen is displayed.

29. Use the mouse or the arrow keys to position the cursor at the end of the *Phone* field. The end of the field is identified by a short vertical line as seen in the illustration.

**Modifying a Custom Report**
Be sure that your cursor is in this position before performing Step 30.

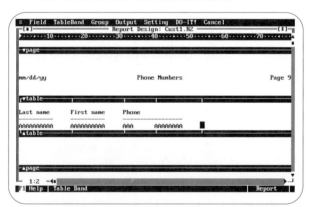

30. Choose TABLEBAND from the menu bar. When the pull-down menu appears, select Insert. Make sure that the cursor is in the right location, then press Enter↵. A new column appears at the cursor position.

31. Use the mouse or the arrow keys to position the cursor on the same line as the other field entries. When the cursor is in the right place it will be directly above the short vertical line at the end of the *Phone* field.

32. Choose FIELD from the menu bar, select Place, then Regular. A list of the fields in your database is displayed. Locate the *Date* field, select it, and press [Enter←] or click OK.

33. The next window displays a list of the formats that can be used to control the appearance of the date in your report. Select format one (mm/dd/yy) and press [Enter←].

34. Check the location of the cursor one more time. If everything is in the correct place, press [Enter←] again. The new field appears.

35. Move the cursor up one line and press the hyphen [[-]] enough times to create a divider line similar to the one below the other column headings.

36. Move the cursor up one more line and type the heading **Purchase Date**. If you want the text to line up with the field entry below, be sure that the letter *P* in *Purchase* is directly above the short vertical divider line. In other words, when you finish, the new field, the dashed divider line, and the heading at the top of the column will all line up on the left.

37. When you finish, press [F2] (DO-IT!) to exit and save your modified form.

### DISPLAYING AND PRINTING THE REPORT

38. Choose REPORT from the menu bar. When the pull-down menu appears, select Output.

39. Load the CUSTOMER database from the list of files that is displayed.

40. Choose Customer Phone List - Master from the list of reports that is displayed, and press [Enter←] or click OK.

41. When the next box appears, select Screen. The contents of your database displays according to the guidelines defined in the Customer Phone List - Master report form. If necessary, use the scroll bars at the left and on the bottom to examine any parts of the report that extend past the edges of the screen.

**The Finished Report**
This is how your completed Custom report should look.

### CREATING INSTANT REPORTS

42. Choose VIEW from the menu bar and select the CUSTOMER database file from the list.

43. When the Database window appears, press [Alt]-[F7]. Paradox prints your data using the Standard report format.

**FINISHING UP**

44. You have completed this tutorial. Press Alt-F8 to clear the desktop and close any files that might be open. Go on to the next activity or exit the program.

## ▶ Q U I C K   R E F E R E N C E

Defining a report format can be time consuming, so Paradox lets you save the formats you create so that you can use them again. You assign each format a name, Paradox attaches it to your database, and saves it on the disk.

When preparing a report with Paradox, you open the REPORT menu, choose Design, and make your choices. Later, if you want to change the report format, open the REPORT menu and choose Change.

### REPORT DESIGN MENU COMMANDS

| Command | Description |
|---------|-------------|
| **Options Menu** | |
| FIELD | These menu choices are used to place (insert), erase, and control the appearance of the data in fields used in a report. |
| TABLEBAND | This menu lets you Insert, Erase, Resize, Move, and Copy columns in the report. |
| GROUPS | (Discussed in Topic 18) |
| OUTPUT | Prints the report (as defined) to the Printer, the Screen, or to a File. In general, this command is identical to the REPORT, Output command on the menu bar. |
| SETTING | Controls the overall format of margins, layout, and print characteristics of your report definition. All of these options have default values that Paradox uses unless you change them. |
| DO-IT! | Exits the Report design screen and saves your work. |
| CANCEL | Exits the Report design screen but *does not* save your work. You can also use this option if you make a mistake and want to start over. |

## ▶ E X E R C I S E S

### EXERCISE 1

### CREATING A REPORT FOR THE EMPLOYEE FILE

1. Create a report named *Employee List* based on the EMPLOYEE database. The finished report should display the *Last name*, *First name*, *Street*, *City*, *State*, and *Zip* fields.

2. View the report on the screen and, if necessary, modify the report to make any necessary corrections.
3. Print the finished report.

**The Completed Employee Report**
This is how your completed Employee report should look.

```
2/18/93                  Phone Numbers                Page    1

Last name    First name    Phone                Purchase Date
----------   ----------    ------------------   -------------
Itwork       Will          407     555-1265      1/10/93
Burnem       Chrispin      415     555-2653      2/12/93
Canbe        Titus         415     555-2731      3/12/93
Roundalot    Liza          404     555-8764      3/05/93
Will         Betty         203     555-1001      1/16/92
Will         Betty         203     555-1001      1/16/92
Cross        Chris         617     555-1002      1/08/92
Time         Lotta         312     555-1003      2/01/92
Driver       Lori          201     555-1004      9/06/92
Dactal       Terry         408     555-1005      8/01/92
Bellum       Sara          201     555-1006      3/06/92
Yet          Seekum        617     555-1007      1/07/92
Dactal       Perry         508     555-1008      6/03/92
Frog         Ura           508     555-1009      1/10/92
Framed       Iben          201     555-1010     10/15/92
```

*Making Calculations*

> **After completing this topic, you will be able to:**
> ■ Create new fields based on calculations from data in other fields using the CALC operator
> ■ Make calculations with functions such as SUM and AVERAGE

You can make calculations using the data stored in two or more Paradox fields using the CALC operator. For example, you can multiply the contents of the *Price* field by the contents of the *Quantity* field to determine the value of inventory. Similarly, you can subtract the date in the *Date_in* field from the date in the *Date_out* field to find out how long an item has been in inventory.

## ▶ P A R A D O X   T U T O R I A L

In this tutorial, you perform a number of calculations using the OVERVIEW database file.

### GETTING STARTED

1. If necessary, set the default drive to drive A (or B).
2. Open the ASK menu and locate the OVERVIEW file.

### USING FUNCTIONS

3. Type **CALC SUM** in the *Qty* field and press [F2] (DO-IT!) to total the *Qty* field of all records. When you are finished viewing the result, press [F8] to close the Answer table.
4. Do not erase the entry in the *Qty* field, but type **Computer** in the *Product* field. Press [F2] (DO-IT!) to total the *Qty* field only for records with *Computer* in the *Product* field.
5. When you are finished, press [F8] to close the Answer table. Then use [← Bksp] to erase the entries in all fields.
6. Move to the *Price* field, and type **CALC AVERAGE**. Press [F2] (DO-IT!) to average the numbers in the *Price* field. When you are finished viewing the result, press [F8] to close the Answer table.
7. Do not erase the entry in the *Price* field, but type **Computer** in the *Product* field. Press [F2] (DO-IT!) to average the *Price* field only for records with *Computer* in the *Product* field.
8. When you are finished, press [F8] to close the Answer table. Then use [← Bksp] to erase the entries in all fields.

**Calculated Numeric Fields**
When you type the command **CALC PRICE*QTY AS TOTAL** in the Query Overview table, Paradox creates a new field called *TOTAL*.

**Calculated Date Fields**
When you type the command **CALC OUT-ORD AS DELAY** in the Query Overview table, Paradox creates a new field called *DELAY*.

## USING CALCULATED FIELDS

9. Place a check mark in the *Product*, *Price*, and *Qty* fields. Type the Example Element PRICE in the *Price* field, move to the *Qty* field, and assign another Example Element called QTY. (Remember, to assign an Example Element, press [F5] first, then type the name.) Move to the next field and type **CALC PRICE*QTY**. Press [F2] to multiply the *Price* and *Qty* fields in each record and show the results in a new field called PRICE*QTY.

10. When you are finished, press [F8] to close the Answer table.

11. Move to the field that contains your formula and add the text *AS TOTAL* to the end. In other words, when you finish, your formula should say **CALC PRICE*QTY AS TOTAL**. Press [F2]. Paradox will multiply the *Price* and *Qty* fields in each record, but this time the new field will be called *TOTAL*.

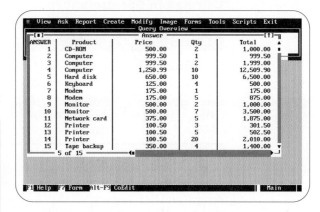

12. Press [Alt]-[F8] to close all windows and clear the desktop.

13. Open the ASK menu and locate the OVERVIEW file.

14. Place a check mark in the *Date_ord*, *Date_out*, and *Product* fields.

15. Type the Example Element OUT in the *Date_out* field, and one named ORD in the *Date_ord* field. Remember to press [F5] before you type the name of the Example Elements.

16. Move to another field and type the formula **CALC OUT-ORD AS DELAY**. Press [F2] (DO-IT!) to list each product name along with the number of days between the date it was ordered and the date it was shipped. The new column will be named *DELAY*.

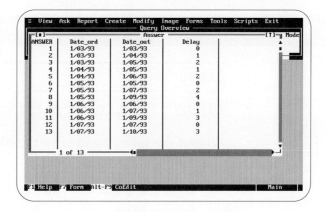

**FINISHING UP**

17. You have completed this tutorial. Press [Alt]-[F8] to close all open files and clear the desktop. Go on to the next activity or exit the program.

## ►QUICK REFERENCE

You can use the functions described in the table "Calculation Operators" to make calculations. For example, to calculate the total of all the numbers in the *Amount* field, you would move to the *Amount* field and use the command CALC SUM.

### Calculation Operators

| Function | Description |
| --- | --- |
| AVERAGE | Calculates the average in a specified numeric field |
| SUM | Calculates the total of the values in a specified numeric field |
| COUNT | Counts the number of records that meet a specified criterion |
| MAX | Displays the largest value in a group |
| MIN | Displays the smallest value in a group |

The Calculation operators cause Paradox to add a new field to the Answer table. If necessary, this new field can be renamed with the AS operator. For example, the formula **CALC PRICE*QTY AS TOTAL** creates a new column that displays the result of the calculation PRICE * QTY. This new column will be named *TOTAL*.

To use calculation operators, first decide which fields need to be used in the calculation. Next, place a unique Example Element in each of these fields, and place a check mark in each field that is to be included in the Answer table (do not place a check mark with the calculation operator). Finally, construct the calculation statement in any column of the Query window. When you press [F2], Paradox displays the results.

If you enter a calculation operator and do not place a check mark in any fields, Paradox will perform a summary calculation on all fields in the database.

## ►EXERCISES

### EXERCISE 1

**MAKING CALCULATIONS IN THE EMPLOYEE FILE**

Answer the following queries based on the EMPLOYEE file.

1. How many employees are in the file?
2. What is the average pay rate for employees?
3. How much pay is the highest paid employee receiving?

4. How much pay is the lowest paid employee receiving?

---

## EXERCISE 2

---

### MAKING CALCULATIONS IN THE TIME FILE

Answer the following queries based on the TIME file.

1. How many employees are in the file?
2. What is the total number of hours worked by all employees?
3. How many employees worked 40 or more hours in any period?
4. How many employees worked less than 40 hours in any period?
5. What is the average number of hours employees are working per period?

# Managing Files

**After completing this topic, you will be able to:**
- Copy entire databases
- Copy selected fields to a new database
- Copy the structure of a database to a new file
- Erase database files with the DELETE command

As the data stored in database files expand, there come times when you need to delete some data that are no longer needed, make backup copies of important files, and even create new databases from those that already exist.

## ▶ P A R A D O X   T U T O R I A L

In this tutorial, you will copy entire files and parts of files. You will then delete those new files from the disk.

**GETTING STARTED**

1. If necessary, set the default drive to drive A (or B).
2. Press [Alt]-[F8] to clear the desktop and close any files that might be open.

**COPYING AN ENTIRE FILE**

3. Open the TOOLS menu, choose Copy, then Table. When the file selection box appears, choose CUSTOMER.
4. When the next box appears, type **NEW1** and press [Enter ←] (or click OK).
5. Open the VIEW menu, locate NEW1, and examine the new table. The new database is the same as the original CUSTOMER database. When you are finished viewing the file, press [Alt]-[F8] to clear the desktop.
6. Open the TOOLS menu, choose More, then ToDOS. The screen clears and a DOS prompt appears.
7. At the DOS prompt, type **DIR CUSTOMER.*** and press [Enter ←]. A list of the files that belong to the CUSTOMER database is displayed. Now type **DIR NEW1.*** and press [Enter ←] to see a list of files that belong to the NEW1 database.
8. Compare the two lists. Notice that files that have similar extensions have the same size, but the date and the time are different. In other

### IMPORTANT NOTE

You should *not* use DOS to copy Paradox files. A Paradox database consists of a group of files called a *family*. If you do not copy all of the files in the family, the new copy of your database may not operate correctly.

### NOTE

At this point Paradox has temporarily loaded a second copy of DOS so that you can enter DOS commands without losing your work in Paradox. When you are finished working in DOS, you will type **EXIT** and press [Enter ←] to redisplay Paradox.

words, Paradox automatically copied all of the files in the family and assigned a new name.

9. When you are finished comparing the lists, type **EXIT** and press $\boxed{\text{Enter} \leftarrow}$. The DOS screen closes and Paradox returns.

## COPYING THE FILE'S STRUCTURE

10. Select CREATE from the menu bar. When the dialog box appears, type **NEW2** and press $\boxed{\text{Enter} \leftarrow}$ to name the new file.

11. When the Create window opens, choose BORROW from the menu bar, then locate the CUSTOMER database from the list of files. Paradox copies the structure from the CUSTOMER database and displays it in the Create: NEW2 window.

12. Press $\boxed{\text{F2}}$ (DO-IT!) to close the window and save the structure of your new file.

13. Open the REPORT menu, choose Output, then Struct from the list of files that displays. Print a Standard report and you will see that the structure of NEW2 is the same as CUSTOMER.

14. Open the VIEW menu. When the file selection box appears, select the NEW2 file. When the table appears, it will be empty. When you are finished, press $\boxed{\text{F8}}$ to close the window.

## COPYING SELECTED FIELDS

15. Select CREATE from the menu bar. When the dialog box appears, type **NEW3** and press $\boxed{\text{Enter} \leftarrow}$ to name the new file.

16. When the Create window opens, choose BORROW from the menu bar, then locate the CUSTOMER database from the list of files. Paradox copies the structure from the CUSTOMER database and displays it in the Create: NEW3 window.

17. Use the arrow keys to move the cursor to the *Id* # field (if it is not already there). Press $\boxed{\text{Del}}$, and the *Id* # field disappears.

18. Move to the *Street* field and press $\boxed{\text{Del}}$ again. Continue to press $\boxed{\text{Del}}$ until only the *Last name* and *First name* fields are left.

> **NOTE**
>
> If you make a mistake, choose CANCEL and go back to Step 15.

19. Press $\boxed{\text{F2}}$ (DO-IT!) to close the window and save the structure of your new file.

20. Open the REPORT menu, choose Output, and then Struct from the list of files. Print a Standard report and you will see that the structure of NEW3 is similar to NEW2 but only contains two fields.

## PRINTING A DIRECTORY OF THE FILES ON YOUR DISK

21. Open the TOOLS menu, choose Info, Inventory, and then Tables. When the dialog box appears, type **A:** (or **B:**) and press $\boxed{\text{Enter} \leftarrow}$ or click OK. A list of the tables on drive A (or B) are displayed.

22. Open the REPORT menu. Choose Output, and select LIST from the list of tables that is displayed. Press $\boxed{\text{Enter} \leftarrow}$ or click OK, then select Printer to print a copy of the database files on your floppy disk. When you are finished, press $\boxed{\text{Alt}}$-$\boxed{\text{F8}}$ to clear the desktop.

## DELETING FILES FROM THE DISK

23. Open the TOOLS menu. Choose Delete, then Table.

24. When the list appears, choose NEW1 and press [Enter←] or click OK. A warning appears at the bottom of the screen. Choose OK. NEW1 and its family will be deleted from your disk.

25. Repeat Step 24 to erase the files NEW2 and NEW3.

**FINISHING UP**

26. You have completed this tutorial. Press [Alt]-[F8] to close all files and clear the desktop. Go on to the next activity or exit the program.

# ▶ QUICK REFERENCE

### Erasing Files
To delete a file family from the disk, open the TOOLS menu, choose Delete, and then Table. The main database file and all of its related files are erased.

### Copying Files
To copy a database file family, open the TOOLS menu, choose Copy, and then Table. When the file list appears, select the file to be copied and press [Enter←] or click OK. Finally, assign a name for the new file and press [Enter←] or click OK.

### Copying File Structures
If you want to create a new file similar to an existing one, you can copy all or part of the existing file's structure to use in the new file. To do so, open the CREATE menu and type a name for the new file. When the Create window appears, choose BORROW, and locate the file that contains the original structure. If necessary, delete any unwanted fields, and press [F2] (DO-IT!).

# ▶ EXERCISES

### EXERCISE 1

**COPYING THE EMPLOYEE FILE**

1. Copy the entire EMPLOYEE file family to a file named E1.
2. Open the new file and print a list of its records.
3. Create another new database based on EMPLOYEE, but only use the *Employee* #, *Last name, First name, Street, City, ST,* and *Zip* fields in the new file. Name this new file E2.
4. Open the new file and print its structure.

## EXERCISE 2

### COPYING THE TIME FILE

1. Copy the entire TIME file family to a file named D1.
2. Open the new file and print a list of its records.
3. Create another new database based on TIME, but only use the *Employee* and *Shift* fields in the new file. Name this new file D2.
4. Open the new file and print its structure.

## EXERCISE 3

### DELETING FILES

1. Delete the E1 file from your disk.
2. Delete the D1 file form your disk.
3. When you are finished, print a list of the files that are still on your floppy disk.

# REVIEW

- You can display records with the VIEW command. Choose VIEW from the menu bar, and when the file list displays, locate the file you want to examine.
- You can specify which fields are to be displayed with the ASK command. Choose ASK from the menu bar, and place a check mark in the field(s) that you need to display. To place a check mark in a field, use the arrow keys to move the cursor to the correct field, then press [F6].
- You can use ASK to filter records by specifying criteria so that only records that meet the criteria are displayed.
- Relational operators such as >, <, and = determine if one item is larger, smaller, or equal to another item.
- The logical operators AND and OR filter records through two or more criteria.
- The logical operator NOT is used to display all records that *do not* match the specified criteria.
- You can automatically replace data in a field with the CHANGETO command.
- The FIND operator locates the first record that meets a specified condition.
- You can print all or part of the data in a database file by creating reports with the REPORT command.
- You can calculate numbers and fields with the CALC operator.
- When you define a calculation in a field you must often use Example Elements. To define an Example Element, press [F5], and type a short name.
- You can total records that have identical entries in one field using the SUM operator.
- To delete files from the disk, open the TOOLS menu, and choose Delete.
- To copy all of the files in a family, open the TOOLS menu, choose Copy, then Table.
- To copy the structure of an open database file, choose CREATE to create a new database. When the Create window displays, choose BORROW. If necessary, you can delete any unwanted fields by pressing [Del].

# QUESTIONS

## FILL IN THE BLANK

1. To display all records, you use the ___View___ command.
2. To display only a specified part of the records, you use the ___Ask___ command.

3. To display only the *Name* and *Address* fields, you would use the command _____.

4. Operators that compare the relative size or order of items are called _____ operators.

5. The greater-than operator is specified with the _____ symbol.

6. Operators that connect criteria so that two or more conditions must be met are called _____ operators.

7. The operator that you would use to be sure both of two conditions were met would be the _____ operator.

8. The operator that you would use to be sure either of two conditions was met would be the _____ operator.

9. To list a record that has *CA* in the *ST* field, you could use the command _____.

10. To find a record that has *Hardy* anywhere in the field, you could use the command _____.

11. To create a new field from calculations performed with data from other fields, you will need to use _____ _____ as place holders in your formula.

12. To use the same filter for a number of commands, it would be easier to use the _____ command.

13. If you want a field to display as part of the answer, you must place a _____ _____ in that field.

14. To mark a field for display, use the arrow keys to move to that field and then press the _____ key.

15. To define a new report format, you use the _____-_____ command sequence.

16. To use an existing report format, you use the _____-_____ command sequence.

17. To copy a family of database files to a new set of files named NEWFILE, you use the _____-_____ command sequence.

## MATCH THE COLUMNS

| | |
|---|---|
| 1. VIEW command | ___ Requires that the criterion not be met |
| 2. ASK command | _\ Displays all records in a database file |
| 3. Relational operators | ___ Totals the numbers in the specified numeric field |
| 4. > | |
| 5. < | *20* Copies file families to a new file |
| 6. >= | ___ Defines a report format |
| 7. <= | ___ Uses a report format |
| 8. Logical operators | *4* Greater than |
| 9. AND | ___ Automatically replaces data in a field |
| 10. OR | ___ Used as a place holder when constructing a formula |
| 11. NOT | |
| 12. REPORT-DESIGN command sequence | ___ Used to perform calculations on the data in two or more fields |

13. REPORT-OUTPUT
    command sequence
14. CHANGETO
    command
15. Example Element
16. CALC operator
17. SUM
18. AVERAGE
19. TOOLS-DELETE
    command sequence
20. TOOLS-COPY
    command sequence
21. FIND operator

_2_ Used to specify which fields are to be
    displayed in the Answer table
___ Requires that both criteria be met
_5_ Less than
_6_ Equal to or greater than
_7_ Equal to or less than
___ Operators used to specify two or more
    criteria
___ Averages the numbers in the specified
    numeric fields
___ Operators that compare two items
___ Finds the first record that meets the
    specified condition
___ Requires that either criterion be met
_12_ Deletes files from the disk

## WRITE OUT THE ANSWERS

1. Describe the two commands you can use to display all or part of the records and explain how they differ from one another.

2. List the steps to display selected fields rather than the entire database.

3. Describe what it means to filter records and explain why this is useful.

4. List and describe six relational operators. Give some examples of how they might be used.

5. Briefly describe the logical operators AND and OR. Give some examples of how they might be used.

6. Give the command you would use to display a record with the date *01/01/94* in the *Date* field. Describe each step of the process.

7. Write out the command that you would use to add 10 percent to all the entries in a numeric field named *Interest*.

8. Describe the steps that you would follow to design a new report format.

9. Describe the steps that you would follow to use an existing report format.

10. List two commands that you can use to manage your Paradox files and briefly describe what each does.

# PROJECTS

## PROJECT 1

### QUERYING THE TITLES DATABASE

Use the TITLES database and print the results of the following queries in the Standard report format.

1. Which titles have had more than one edition?
2. What is the average list price?
3. How many titles are in the Science category?
4. Which hard cover text(s) have a list price higher than $30?
5. Which paperback text(s) have a list price higher than $30?
6. What is the highest-priced paperback title?
7. What book by Franks is in the Science category?
8. What paperback book is in the third edition?
9. What is the average price of the paperback texts?
10. What is the average price of the hard cover texts?
11. How many titles are in their first edition?
12. How many titles are in their third edition?

## PROJECT 2

### QUERYING THE SALES DATABASE

Use the SALES database file and print the results of the following queries in the Standard report format.

1. Which ISBNs had sales in trade of at least 5,000 copies?
2. What are the total trade sales? The average?
3. Which ISBNs had sales of at least 3,000 copies in trade and 1,000 copies in education?
4. What were the total spring sales for Trade and Education? Fall sales?
5. What was the average spring sales for International and Mail? Fall sales?
6. What are the total sales for Trade?
7. What are the total sales for Educational?
8. What are the total sales for Mail?

## PROJECT 3

### PREPARING A REPORT FOR THE TITLES FILE

Prepare a report named TITLEREP for the TITLES database that lists just the ISBN, title, author, edition, version, and price. Use this report to print out the file.

# Sorting & Indexing Databases

## Sorting Records

**After completing this topic, you will be able to:**
- Sort databases with the MODIFY-SORT command sequence
- Sort files on both primary and secondary fields
- Sort databases in descending order

When you sort a file, Paradox rearranges the records and saves them to a new file on the disk in the order that you specify. For example, you can sort the file so that names are arranged alphabetically or so that a given set of numbers is arranged in ascending or descending order. Since these data are stored in fields, you specify which fields you want arranged and in what order you want the data sorted.

When you specify one field to use, you are designating it as the primary sort field. If two records in the database have the same information in the primary sort field, you can specify a secondary field that can be used to break the tie. If two records in the secondary field are identical, you can specify a third field to break the tie, and so on. The primary field is sorted first. If you are sorting a list of names in the original file, the primary key sorts it so that all the names are in ascending or descending alphabetical order. Ideally, a primary field stores unique information such as a driver's license number, an employee number, or a social security number. But often, this field does not meet your needs, and in many cases, it will not even exist.

For example, when you sort a file by last name, the file may have more than one person with the same last name. In these cases, you must use a secondary key, like the first name, to break ties.

## ▶ PARADOX TUTORIAL

In this tutorial, you will sort the MEMBERS database file.

### GETTING STARTED

1. If necessary, set the default drive to drive A (or B).

## SORTING A FILE IN ASCENDING ORDER

**The Original CUSTOMER File**
The last names in the original CUSTOMER file are arranged randomly based on the order in which they were entered.

2. Open the VIEW menu and select the CUSTOMER file. Notice how the last names are in random order. When you are finished, press F8 to close the View window.

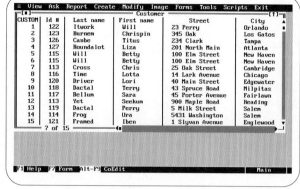

3. Open the MODIFY menu and select Sort. When the file selection box appears, locate and select CUSTOMER.

4. When the next selection box displays, choose New, type **ASCEND1** in the dialog box, and press Enter←┘ or click OK.

5. Use the arrow keys to move the cursor next to the *Last name* field. Type **1** and press F2 (DO-IT!). You will see a "Sorting" indicator at the bottom of the screen.

6. After a few seconds, a new list appears. This new list is named ASCEND1 and is arranged alphabetically by last name in ascending order.

7. When you are finished, press Alt - F8 to close all open files and clear the desktop.

**The CUSTOMER File Sorted on the Last Name Field**
This is what the new file (ASCEND1) will look like when it is sorted on the *Last name* field.

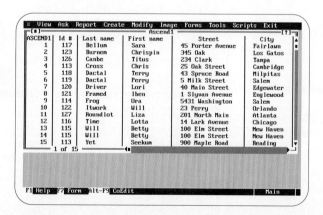

## SORTING A FILE USING PRIMARY AND SECONDARY FIELDS

8. Open the MODIFY menu and select Sort. When the file selection box appears, locate and select CUSTOMER.

9. When the next selection box displays, choose New, type **ASCEND2** in the dialog box, and press Enter←┘ or click OK.

10. Use the arrow keys to move the cursor next to the *Last name* field and type **1**. Move the cursor to the *First name* field and type **2**. Finally, press F2 (DO-IT!). You will see a "Sorting" indicator at the bottom of the screen.

11. After a few seconds, a new list appears. This new list is named ASCEND2 and it is arranged alphabetically by last name in ascending order. However, if the last name is the same in two or more records, the records will be arranged according to the first name.

12. When you are finished, press Alt - F8 to close all open files and clear the desktop.

**The CUSTOMER File Sorted on the Last Name and First Name Fields**

When you sort the file based on the *Last name* and *First name* fields (ASCEND2), ties in the last name are broken and arranged in order based on the contents of the *First name* field.

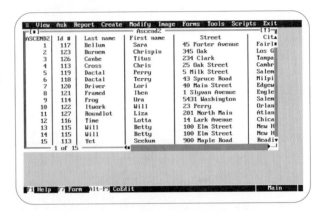

## SORTING A FILE IN DESCENDING ORDER

13. Open the MODIFY menu and select Sort. When the file selection box appears, locate and select CUSTOMER.

14. When the next selection box displays, choose New, type **DE-SCEND1** in the dialog box, and press Enter ↵ or click OK.

15. Use the arrow keys to move the cursor next to the *Last name* field, type **1D**, and press F2 (DO-IT!). You will see a "Sorting" indicator at the bottom of the screen.

16. After a few seconds, a new list appears. This new list is named DESCEND1 and is arranged in *reverse* alphabetical order by last name.

17. When you are finished, press Alt - F8 to close all open files and clear the desktop.

**The File Sorted on the Last Name Field in Descending Order**

This is what the new file (DESCEND1) will look like when it is sorted on the *Last name* field in descending order.

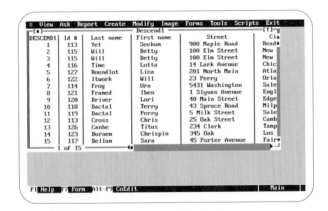

## FINISHING UP

18. You have completed this tutorial. If necessary, press Alt - F8 to close all open files and clear the desktop. Go on to the next activity or exit the program.

To sort a file, you use the MODIFY-SORT command sequence. The specified fields are used to change the order of all records in the file. For example, to sort a file on the *Last name* field to a new file named TEMP, you would select the MODIFY-SORT command sequence, and when the next window opens, number the fields from most important to least important. For example, to sort a file on last, first, and middle names, type **1** next to *Last name*, **2** next to *First name*, and **3** next to *Middle*.

Normally, files are sorted in ascending order. To sort a file in descending order, type **D** next to the number. For example, to sort a file in descending order by last name, type **1D** next to *Last name*.

### EXERCISE 1

#### SORTING THE EMPLOYEE FILE

1. Open the MODIFY menu and select Sort. When the file selection box appears, locate and select EMPLOYEE.
2. When the next selection box displays, choose New, type **EMPSRT1** in the dialog box, and press [Enter ←] or click OK.
3. Sort the file in ascending order by last name.
4. Make a printout of the sorted file.
5. Press [Alt]-[F8] to clear the desktop.

### EXERCISE 2

#### SORTING THE EMPLOYEE FILE (CONTINUED)

1. Open the MODIFY menu and select Sort. When the file selection box appears, locate and select EMPLOYEE.
2. When the next selection box displays, choose New, type **EMPSRT2** in the dialog box, and press [Enter ←] or click OK.
3. Sort the file in ascending order by last name and employee number.
4. Make a printout of the sorted file.
5. Press [Alt]-[F8] to clear the desktop.

### EXERCISE 3

#### SORTING THE TIME FILE

1. Open the MODIFY menu and select Sort. When the file selection box appears, locate and select TIME.
2. Sort the file on the employee number in descending order to a new file named DEPTORD.
3. Make a printout of the sorted file.
4. Press [Alt]-[F8] to clear the desktop.

# Assigning Key Fields

After completing this topic, you will be able to:
- Explain the advantage of using key fields as compared to sorting
- Assign a key to more than one field

Many database programs use the word *index* to describe what Paradox calls a *key* or *key field*. Anytime key fields are marked, Paradox displays the records, in order, based on those fields. Ideally, a key field contains only unique values. In fact, if only one key is assigned, it *must* be the first field of your database and it *must* contain unique entries.

Sorting is not always the best way to arrange a file. It can take a long time to sort a large file, and a file can be sorted in only one order at a time. For example, the post office gives reduced rates for mailings presorted in zip code order. If you sort a name and address file by last name, you would need to re-sort it by zip code before printing mailing labels. To maintain lists like these you would need separate files, each sorted differently, and any time you have more than one file that contains essentially the same data, you are wasting valuable disk space.

**An Indexed File**

In this illustration, a database file has been indexed by last name. The actual file remains in its original order, but the index causes the file to display in order by last name.

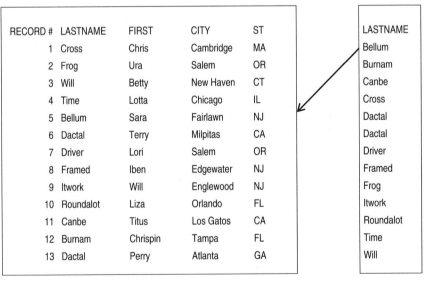

| RECORD # | LASTNAME | FIRST | CITY | ST |
|---|---|---|---|---|
| 1 | Cross | Chris | Cambridge | MA |
| 2 | Frog | Ura | Salem | OR |
| 3 | Will | Betty | New Haven | CT |
| 4 | Time | Lotta | Chicago | IL |
| 5 | Bellum | Sara | Fairlawn | NJ |
| 6 | Dactal | Terry | Milpitas | CA |
| 7 | Driver | Lori | Salem | OR |
| 8 | Framed | Iben | Edgewater | NJ |
| 9 | Itwork | Will | Englewood | NJ |
| 10 | Roundalot | Liza | Orlando | FL |
| 11 | Canbe | Titus | Los Gatos | CA |
| 12 | Burnam | Chrispin | Tampa | FL |
| 13 | Dactal | Perry | Atlanta | GA |

| LASTNAME |
|---|
| Bellum |
| Burnam |
| Canbe |
| Cross |
| Dactal |
| Dactal |
| Driver |
| Framed |
| Frog |
| Itwork |
| Roundalot |
| Time |
| Will |

**The database file**                                    **Index (key field)**

**NOTE**

If possible, assign key fields when you define a database structure for the first time. If you restructure a database and add key fields, you could lose data.

Once you have indicated key fields, Paradox automatically keeps everything up to date. If you add records, insert records, delete records, or change the data in a field, everything rearranges automatically as specified by the key.

In general, keys prevent duplicate records within a field, keep the table sorted according to the values in that field, and establish *relationships* between otherwise separate databases. Every Paradox database should have at least one key field.

In this tutorial, you will add keys to the CUSTOMER database.

## GETTING STARTED

1. If necessary, set the default drive to drive A (or B).

## ASSIGNING A KEY FIELD

2. Open the MODIFY menu, choose Restructure, and locate the CUSTOMER database file.

3. When the Restructure window opens, use the arrow keys to move to the Field Type columns for the *Id #* field. Type an asterisk (*) after the existing Field Type definition and press [F2] (DO-IT!).

**Adding a Key to an Existing File**
This illustration shows the Restructure window. This is the screen that you will use to assign key fields to a database.

```
≡  Borrow  JustFamily  FileFormat  DO-IT!  Cancel
┌─[▪]──────────────── Restructure: Customer ────────────────[‡]─┐
│STRUCT │      Field Name      │ Field Type │▲│                  │
│    1  │ Id #                 │ A3*  ◄     │▪│ ──── FIELD TYPES ────
│    2  │ Last name            │ A10        │ │ A_: Alphanumeric.  │
│    3  │ First name           │ A10        │ │ All characters up to│
│    4  │ Street               │ A17        │ │ max of 255 (ex: A9).│
│    5  │ City                 │ A10        │ │                     │
│    6  │ ST                   │ A2         │ │ M_: Memo. Alphanumeric│
│    7  │ Zip                  │ A5         │ │ characters, 240 maximum│
│    8  │ Area                 │ A3         │ │ display in table view.│
│    9  │ Phone                │ A8         │ │                     │
│   10  │ Date                 │ D          │ │ N: Numbers with or  │
│   11  │ Age                  │ N          │ │ without decimal digits.│
│   12  │ Remarks              │ M10        │ │                     │
│       │                      │            │ │ $: Currency amounts.│
│       │                      │            │ │                     │
│       │                      │            │ │ D: Dates in the form│
│       │                      │            │ │ mn/dd/yy, dd-mon-yy,│
│       │                      │            │ │ dd.mn.yy, or yy.mn.dd.│
│       │                      │            │▼│                     │
│       │                      │            │ │ Use * for key fields│
│       │                      │            │ │ (ex: N*). Not memos.│
├──────────────────────────────────────────────────────────────┤
│F1 Help                                            │Restructure│ │
└───────────────────────────────────────────────────────────────┘
```

## HANDLING KEY VIOLATIONS

If two records of a keyed field contain the same information, this is called a *key violation*.

4. After a few seconds a new window opens. The new window displays all of the records that have duplicate entries. For example, if there are two or more records with 115 in the *Id #* field, only the *duplicated* records (not the original records) appear in the Key Viol window.

5. Press [F9] (EDIT) and change the Id number for Record one to **124** and the Id number for Record two to **125**. When you are finished, press [F2] (DO_IT!).

6. Open the TOOLS menu, choose More, and then Add. When the Source table window opens, choose KEYVIOL, and press [Enter ↵] (or click OK).

7. When the Target table window opens, choose CUSTOMER, then select Update. The modified entries are copied from the KEYVIOL table into the CUSTOMER file.

**NOTE**

If you only assign one key field, it must be the *first* field in the structure definition.

8. You will now see your restructured database, in order, according to the new key field. Press [Alt]-[F8] to close all windows and clear the desktop.

## ASSIGNING A KEY TO MORE THAN ONE FIELD

If you assign a key to two (or more) fields, you can have duplicate entries in the first field. In other words, two (or more) records could store the number 100 in the first keyed field if all of the second keyed fields are different.

When you assign more than one key field, you must choose them from the top to the bottom in the structure window. The first keyed field would be the first field, the second keyed field would be the second, and so on. In other words, when assigning key fields, you cannot skip any fields in the structure definition window.

9. Open the MODIFY menu, choose Restructure, and locate the PURCHASE database file. If another menu appears, select OK and continue.

10. When the Restructure window opens, type an asterisk (*) after the existing Field Type definition for the *Id #* and *Date* fields. When you finish, press [F2] (DO-IT!).

11. After a few seconds a new window opens. The new window displays your restructured database, in order, according to the new key fields. Notice that when the Id numbers are the same, the records are put in order according to the *Date* field. When you are finished, press [Alt]-[F8] to close all windows and clear the desktop.

**The Keyed PURCHASE Database**
This is what your PURCHASE file will look like after it has been keyed on the *Id #* field.

```
≡  View  Ask  Report  Create  Modify  Image  Forms  Tools  Scripts  Exit
┌─[■]────────────────────────── Purchase ──────────────────[↑]─┐
│PURCHASE│ ID#  │   Date   │    Item Description    │  Amount  │■
│    1   │ 114  │ 10/31/93 │ Large Pocket Watch     │   99.97  │■
│    2   │ 115  │  4/12/93 │ Calico Cat             │    9.95  │
│    3   │ 115  │  3/03/94 │ White Queen Doll       │   29.95  │
│    4   │ 116  │  5/05/93 │ Calico Cat             │    9.95  │
│    5   │ 117  │  9/12/94 │ Very small Table       │   13.95  │
│    6   │ 118  │ 11/16/93 │ Flamingo Croquet Set   │   57.77  │
│    7   │ 119  │  8/04/94 │ Red Queen Doll         │   39.95  │
│    8   │ 120  │  1/04/93 │ Gingham Dog            │   14.95  │
│    9   │ 120  │  8/14/93 │ Tea Set                │   39.95  │
│   10   │ 121  │  6/04/94 │ Calico Cat             │    9.95  │
│   11   │ 121  │  7/10/94 │ Top Hat (size 6-7/8)   │   59.75  │
│   12   │ 122  │  4/10/93 │ White Rabbit (back order) │ 29.95 │
│   13   │ 123  │  4/19/92 │ Chess Board            │   39.95  │
│   14   │ 123  │  3/03/93 │ Cheshire Cat (incomplete) │ 11.50 │
│   15   │ 123  │  3/17/93 │ White Rabbit (back order) │ 29.95 │▼
└──────── 1 of 15 ──────────◀■────────────────────────────▶──┘

F1 Help  F2 Form  Alt-F9 CoEdit                              Main
```

## EDITING A DATABASE THAT HAS KEY FIELDS

If you make an error while editing information in a database that has key fields, Paradox may replace (destroy) existing records without any warning.

To eliminate this problem, you should use the CoEDIT mode (rather than EDIT) to change data in keyed files.

12. Open the VIEW menu and locate the PURCHASE database file.

13. When the table appears, press [F9] (EDIT), use the arrow keys to move to the bottom of the file, then add the following record. Notice that the Id number (114) and the date (10/31/93) are the same as the existing record number one.

| Id number: | 114 |
| Date: | 10/31/93 |
| Item description: | Jabberwocky Doll |
| Amount: | 27.99 |
| Payment method: | Check |

14. Press [F2] (DO-IT!). Paradox replaces record number one with your new entry. Effectively, Paradox makes the change without your permission. When you finish viewing the data, press [Alt]-[F8] to close all windows and clear the desktop.

**The Changed PURCHASE Database**
This is what the PURCHASE database will contain after you perform Step 14. Notice that the new record was not *added* to the database, it *replaced* the existing record number one. Compare this illustration to the previous one.

```
≡  View  Ask  Report  Create  Modify  Image  Forms  Tools  Scripts  Exit
┌─[■]──────────────────── Purchase ────────────────────[↑]─┐
│PURCHASE│ ID# │   Date   │      Item Description      │Amount│
│    1   │ 114 │ 10/31/93 │ Jabberwocky Doll          │ 27.99 ■│
│    2   │ 115 │  4/12/93 │ Calico Cat                │  9.95 │
│    3   │ 115 │  3/03/94 │ White Queen Doll          │ 29.95 │
│    4   │ 116 │  5/05/93 │ Calico Cat                │  9.95 │
│    5   │ 117 │  9/12/94 │ Very small Table          │ 13.95 │
│    6   │ 118 │ 11/16/93 │ Flamingo Croquet Set      │ 57.77 │
│    7   │ 119 │  8/04/94 │ Red Queen Doll            │ 39.95 │
│    8   │ 120 │  1/04/93 │ Gingham Dog               │ 14.95 │
│    9   │ 120 │  8/14/93 │ Tea Set                   │ 39.95 │
│   10   │ 121 │  6/04/94 │ Calico Cat                │  9.95 │
│   11   │ 121 │  7/10/94 │ Top Hat (size 6-7/8)      │ 59.75 │
│   12   │ 122 │  4/10/93 │ White Rabbit (back order) │ 29.95 │
│   13   │ 123 │  4/19/92 │ Chess Board               │ 39.95 │
│   14   │ 123 │  3/03/93 │ Cheshire Cat (incomplete) │ 11.50 │
│   15   │ 123 │  3/17/93 │ White Rabbit (back order) │ 29.95 ▼│
└──────── 1 of 15 ──────◀█─────────────────────────────►▼─┘

F1 Help  F7 Form  Alt-F9 CoEdit                          Main
```

15. Open the VIEW menu and locate the PURCHASE database again.

16. This time, when the table appears, press [Alt]-[F9] (CoEDIT) rather than [F9] (EDIT). Finally, use the arrow keys to move to the bottom of the file and add the following record. Once again, notice that the Id number (114) and date (10/31/93) are the same as the existing record number one.

| Id number: | 114 |
| Date: | 10/31/93 |
| Item description: | Large Pocket Watch |
| Amount: | 99.97 |
| Payment method: | Cash |

17. Press [F2] (DO-IT!) to finish. This time Paradox displays a warning that says the key already exists. Press the spacebar to return to the CoEDIT mode, and use the arrow keys to move back to the duplicate entry. Change the Id number so that it reads **123** and press [F2] again.

18. This time, because the entries in the first field are different, Paradox adds the new entry correctly. When you are finished viewing the data, press [Alt]-[F8] to clear the desktop.

## CREATING A SECONDARY INDEX

Often it will be convenient to maintain a database with the records in one order and to use it in another. For example, it may be convenient to edit a mailing list with the entries in last name order, but it may be necessary to print the information in zip code order to save on mailing costs. In other words, Secondary indexes can be used to temporarily change the order of the records in a database.

In the following steps you will add a secondary index to the CUSTOMER database.

19. Open the VIEW menu and when the list of files appears, choose CUSTOMER.
20. Open the IMAGE menu and choose OrderTable. Move the cursor to the *Zip* field and press [Enter ←]. When the Indexes box appears, press [Enter ←]. When the next box appears, click OK.
21. After a few seconds, the table will be displayed in ascending order according to zip code.
22. Print a copy of the modified file.

**FINISHING UP**

23. You have completed this tutorial. Press [Alt]-[F8] to close all open files and to clear the desktop. Go on to the next activity or exit the program.

## QUICK REFERENCE

You should assign key fields when you define your database for the first time, but if you need to assign keys to an existing database, you can use the MODIFY-RESTRUCTURE command sequence.

To assign a key, open the file, use the arrow keys to move to the Field Type column of the structure definition window, and then type an asterisk (*) after the Field Type definition. When you finish, press [F2] to close the structure definition window.

In general, keys prevent duplicate records within a field, keep the table sorted according to the values in that field, and establish *relationships* between otherwise separate databases.

Every Paradox database should have at least one key field.

If you assign a key to two (or more) fields, you can have duplicate entries in the first field, but you must choose the fields from the top to the bottom in the structure window. In other words, you cannot skip any fields in the structure definition window.

If a data entry error is made while editing information in a keyed database, Paradox may replace (destroy) existing records without any warning. You should use the CoEDIT mode (rather than EDIT) to change data in keyed files to eliminate this problem.

### Handling Key Violations
If you add keys to an existing database file and two or more keyed fields contain the same information, a *key violation* occurs. To correct a key violation, edit the duplicated records, then use the ADD command to put them back in the original database file.

### Secondary Indexes
Secondary Indexes can be used to temporarily change the order of the records in a database. To establish a Secondary Index, open the IMAGE menu, choose OrderTable, and move the cursor to the field that will establish the order.

## EXERCISE 1

### INDEXING THE EMPLOYEE FILE

1. Open the MODIFY menu and choose Restructure. When the file list displays, choose the EMPLOYEE database.
2. Assign a key to the *Employee* # field.
3. Print a list of the *Employee* #, *Last name*, *First name*, and *Department* fields.

## EXERCISE 2

### INDEXING THE TIME FILE

1. Restructure the TIME database by assigning keys to the *Week of* and the *Employee* # fields.
2. Print a list of the keyed file.

# REVIEW

- When you sort a file, Paradox rearranges the records and saves them to a new file on the disk in the order that you specify.
- When you specify which field is to be used, you are designating it as the primary sort field. If two records in the database have the same information in the primary sort field, you can specify a secondary field to break the tie.
- To sort a file in descending order, type **D** as part of the sort order indicator. In other words, to sort field one in descending order, you would type **1D** next to the field name.
- Sorting is not always the best way to arrange a file. It can take a long time to sort a large file, and a file can be sorted in only one order at a time.
- Many database programs use the word *index* to describe what Paradox calls a *key* or *key field*. Any time key fields are marked, Paradox displays the records, in order, based on those fields. Ideally, a key field contains only unique values. In fact, if only one key is assigned, it *must* be the first field of your database and it *must* contain unique entries.
- Once you have indicated key fields, Paradox automatically keeps everything up to date. If you add records, insert records, delete records, or change the data in a field, everything rearranges automatically as specified by the key.
- Keys prevent duplicate records within a field in order to keep the table sorted according to the values in that field and to establish *relationships* between otherwise separate databases. Every Paradox database should have at least one key field.
- If possible, assign key fields when you define a database structure for the first time. If you restructure a database and add key fields, you could lose data.
- If you add keys to an existing database file and two or more keyed fields contain the same information, a *key violation* occurs. To correct a key violation, edit the duplicated records and use the ADD command to put them back in the original database file.
- Secondary Indexes can be used to temporarily change the order of the records in a database. To establish a Secondary Index, open the IMAGE menu, choose OrderTable, and move the cursor to the field that will establish the order.

# QUESTIONS

## FILL IN THE BLANK

1. Many database programs use the word *index* to describe what Paradox calls a _____ or a _____.

2. To sort a file on its *Id #* field to a new file named NEW, you would use the _____ command sequence.
3. Keys are used to prevent _____ records within a field.
4. _____ is not always the best way to arrange a file.
5. If you assign a key to more than one field, you must choose the fields _____.
6. To temporarily place a database in a different order, you would use a _____ _____.

---

## WRITE OUT THE ANSWERS

---

1. Describe how you would sort a file in ascending order by last name to a new file named NEWFILE. Describe how you would do so in descending order.
2. Describe how you would assign a key to the *Name* field of a database. Describe how you would assign a key to both the *Name* and *City* fields.
3. What is the difference between sorting and keying a file? Describe ways in which keying might be better for you.
4. What is a *key violation*?
5. List the steps that you would follow to recover from a key violation.
6. Describe a Secondary Index. Under what conditions would you use a Secondary Index?

---

## CHAPTER 4 | PROJECTS

---

### PROJECT 1

---

#### SORTING AND KEYING THE TITLES DATABASE

1. Locate the TITLES database file.
2. Sort the file to a file named CATEGORY based on the *Category* field.
3. Print a list of the sorted CATEGORY file.
4. Key the TITLES file on the *ISBN* field and print a list of the keyed file.

---

### PROJECT 2

---

#### SORTING AND KEYING THE SALES DATABASE

1. Locate the SALES database file.
2. Sort the file to a file named ISBN based on the *ISBN* field.
3. Print a list of the sorted ISBN file.
4. Key the SALES file on the *ISBN* and *Period* fields. Print a list of the keyed file.

# Working with Multiple Database Files

---

## Relating Database Files

---

**After completing this topic, you will be able to:**
- Query related files
- Change the display order of the data in a table using the ROTATE command

The big advantage of a database management program is that it lets you work with more than one file at the same time. If the files have a common field, you can link the data in two or more tables with *Example Elements*. After you place the Example Elements in the fields that link the tables, you can construct a *query statement* using two or more query forms. There is no limit (other than the RAM in your computer) to the number of tables that can be linked.

You can place two (or more) query forms in the workspace by using the ASK command more than one time. The order of the forms in the workspace does not matter, but remember, checked fields from the query form on the top of the workspace become the left-hand fields in the answer table. Fields in the second form display to the right of the fields in the first form, and so on. You can rearrange the fields later using the IMAGE menu options and the Ctrl-R (rotate) command.

**Related Database Files**
The database shown here contains two files. The first file is used to store customer names and the second their purchases. Because they share a common *Id #* field, you can make queries on information such as the first name, last name, and the amount for Id number 101.

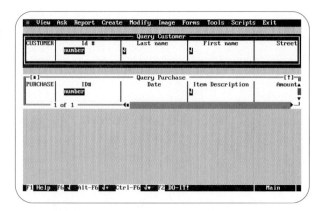

In this tutorial, you will establish a relationship between the MEMBERS and CHARGES database files, then query both files at the same time.

### GETTING STARTED

1. If necessary, set the default drive to drive A (or B).

### QUERYING THE RELATED DATABASES

2. Open the ASK menu and locate the CUSTOMER table.
3. When the Query window appears, move the cursor to the *Id #* field. Press [F6] to place a check mark in this field.
4. Press [F5] and type the Example Element **NUMBER** in the *Id #* field.
5. Place a check mark in the *Last name* and *First name* fields.
6. Open the ASK menu again and locate the PURCHASE file.
7. When the Query window appears, move the cursor to the *Id #* field, press [F5], and type the Example Element **NUMBER** in this field.
8. Move the cursor to the *Item description* field and press [F6]. A check mark appears in the field.
9. Press [F2] (DO-IT!). A list of all customers and their purchases appears. The records will be in order according to their Id number. When you are finished, press [F8] to close the Answer table.

**The Linked CUSTOMER and PURCHASE Files**
This is what your screen displays when you have completed Step 9.

10. Move the cursor to the *Amount* field in the PURCHASE Query window. Press [F6] to enter a check mark, then type **>29.00** next to the check mark. Press [F2] (DO-IT!). An Answer table appears that displays a list of all customers and their purchases, but only if their purchase was greater than $29.00.

**The Linked CUSTOMER and PURCHASE Files (continued)**

This is what your screen displays when you have completed Step 10.

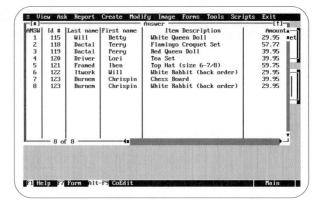

11. Press [F8] to close the Answer table.

### SAVING A QUERY WINDOW

12. Open the SCRIPTS menu and choose QuerySave. When the dialog box appears, type the query name **PURCH** and press [Enter ←] or click OK.

13. Press [Alt]-[F8] to clear the desktop.

### USING A QUERY THAT HAS BEEN SAVED

14. Open the SCRIPTS menu and choose Play. Press [Enter ←] (or click OK) and locate the PURCH file.

15. Press [Enter ←] (or click OK) again. The query that was saved in Step 12 reappears. To display the data requested by the Query window, press [F2] (DO-IT!).

### CHANGING A QUERY THAT HAS BEEN SAVED

16. Press [F8] to close the Answer table.

17. Move the cursor to the *Amount* field in the PURCHASE Query window, use [← Bksp] to erase the entry there, and change it to **>49.00**.

18. Open the SCRIPTS menu and choose QuerySave. When the dialog box appears, type the query name **PURCH** and press [Enter ←] or click OK. When the next box appears, select Replace to update the PURCH script.

19. Press [F2] to display the data from the new query.

**The Linked CUSTOMER and PURCHASE Files (continued)**

This is what your screen displays when you have completed Step 19.

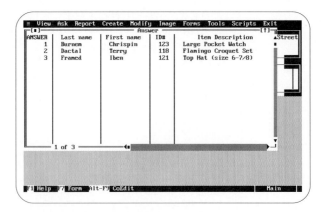

## CHANGING THE DISPLAY ORDER OF THE FIELDS

20. Use the arrow keys to move the cursor to the *First name* field. Press [Ctrl]-[R] (rotate) and the *First name* field moves to column five of the display.

21. Move the cursor to the *Last name* field and press [Ctrl]-[R] again. This time the *Last name* field moves to column five of the display.

22. Move the cursor to the *Item description* field and press [Ctrl]-[R]. When you are finished, the first column should be the *Id #*, followed by the *Amount*, *First name*, *Last name*, and *Item description*, as shown in the illustration below.

**The Answer Table After Rotating the Fields**
This is what your screen displays when you have completed Step 22.

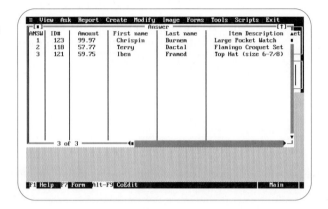

23. When you finish viewing the data, press [Alt]-[F8] to clear the desktop.

### FINISHING UP

24. You have completed this tutorial. Go on to the next activity or exit the program.

---

# ►QUICK REFERENCE

Two database files can be related if they share a common field. To create this relationship, you link the data in two or more tables with *Example Elements.* After the Example Elements are placed in the fields that link the tables, you can construct a *query statement* that is made up of two or more query forms.

After you construct the query forms, you can save them with the SCRIPTS- QUERYSAVE command sequence. Saved query forms can be reused at any time by opening the SCRIPTS menu and choosing Play.

You can also change the order of the columns in a display by pressing [Ctrl]-[R]. Each time you press [Ctrl]-[R] the current column (the column where the cursor is located) moves to the last column of the Answer table.

> E X E R C I S E S

## EXERCISE 1

### RELATING THE EMPLOYEE AND TIME FILES

1. Open the ASK menu and locate the EMPLOYEE file.
2. Move the cursor to the *Employee #* field, and enter the Example Element **NUMBER**.
3. Place a check mark in the *Last name* and *First name* fields.
4. Open the ASK menu and locate the TIME file.
5. Move the cursor into the *Employee #* field, and enter the Example Element **NUMBER**.
6. Place a check mark in the *Employee #*, *Hours*, and *Shift* fields.
7. Press F2 (DO-IT!).
8. Print a list of the records.

**The Linked EMPLOYEE and TIME Files**

```
2/25/93                      Standard Report                     Page    1
Last Name    First Name   Employee #          Hours    Shift

Beef         Sida         107                 10.00    3
Beef         Sida         107                 40.00    1
Binone       Ida          110                 30.00    3
Binone       Ida          110                 40.00    1
DeVille      Marguerite   112                 40.00    1
Dune         Lorna        108                 25.00    3
Dune         Lorna        108                 40.00    3
Earl         Duka         109                 40.00    1
Earl         Duka         109                 40.00    3
Minute       Ina          105                 20.00    3
Minute       Ina          105                 25.00    1
Minute       Justa        113                 40.00    1
Rose         Lieca        111                 20.00    2
Rose         Lieca        111                 40.00    1
Will         Betty        106                 20.00    1
Will         Betty        106                 37.00    2
```

# Joining Database Files

> **After completing this topic, you will be able to:**
> ■ Combine two database files into a single new file

If you have two files with a common field, you can combine them into a single new file if both have the same value in a specified common field. For example, both your CUSTOMER and PURCHASE files contain a common *Id #* field. These common fields can be used to link the two separate files and create one new file.

**Joined Database Files**

This database contains two files but each has an *Id #* field that is common to both. You can use that common field to combine the two files into a new file that contains all (or some) of the fields from the two original files.

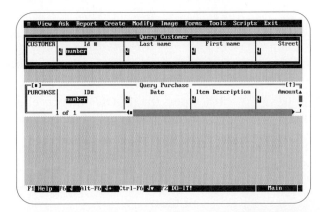

## ▶ P A R A D O X  T U T O R I A L

In this tutorial, you will combine the CUSTOMER and PURCHASE database files to form two new files named NEWFILE1 and NEWFILE2.

**GETTING STARTED**

1. If necessary, set the default drive to A (or B).

**OPENING FILES**

2. Open the ASK menu and locate the CUSTOMER database.
3. Move the cursor to the first column of the Query window (if it is not already there) and press F6 . A check mark should appear in all of the other fields.
4. Move the cursor to the *Id #* field, press F5 , and type the Example Element **NUMBER**.
5. Open the ASK menu again, and this time select the PURCHASE database.

6. Move the cursor to the first column of the Query window (if it is not already there) and press F6 . A check mark should appear in all of the other fields.

7. Move the cursor to the *Id #* field, press F5 , and type the Example Element NUMBER again.

8. While the cursor is still in the *Id #* field, press F6 to remove the check mark from the *Id #* field in the PURCHASE Query window.

## JOINING THE FILES

9. Press F2 (DO-IT!). An Answer table opens. Only the records that have matching numbers in the *Id #* field are included.

**The NEWFILE1 File**
All fields from PURCHASE and CUSTOMER are combined into the new file.

10. Open the TOOLS menu, choose Rename, and then select Table. Select ANSWER from the list that appears and change its name to NEWFILE1.

11. Open the REPORT menu and print NEWFILE1 using the Standard Report format.

12. When you are finished, press Alt - F8 to clear the desktop and close all files.

**NOTE**

If you do not rename the Answer table, its data will be lost the next time a query is made.

## JOINING SELECTED FIELDS

13. Open the ASK menu and locate the CUSTOMER database.

14. Use the arrow keys to move the cursor and place a check mark in the *Id #*, *Last name*, and *First name* fields.

15. Move to the *Id #* field and type the Example Element NUMBER.

16. Open the ASK menu again and locate the PURCHASE database.

17. Use the arrow keys to move the cursor and place a check mark in the *Item description* and *Amount* fields.

18. Move to the *Id #* field and type the Example Element NUMBER.

19. Press F2 (DO-IT!). An Answer table opens. The new table contains the checked fields from both files, but only the records that have matching numbers in the *Id #* field are included.

**The NEWFILE2 File**

Only the specified fields from CUSTOMER and PURCHASE are included in NEWFILE2.

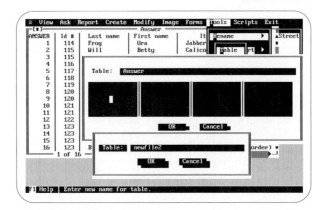

20. Open the TOOLS menu, choose Rename, and then select Table. Select ANSWER from the list that appears and change its name to NEWFILE2.

21. Open the REPORT menu and print NEWFILE2 using the Standard Report format.

**FINISHING UP**

22. You have completed this tutorial. Press ⌐Alt¬-⌐F8¬ to clear the desktop and close all open files. Go on to the next activity or exit the program.

# ▶ QUICK REFERENCE

- You can combine files by opening a Query window for each file, placing a check mark in the fields that are to be included, and assigning an Example Element to the field that links the two databases.
- When the new table appears, use the TOOLS-RENAME-TABLE command sequence to create a new file that only contains the fields and records you requested.

# ▶ EXERCISES

## EXERCISE 1

### JOINING THE EMPLOYEE AND TIME FILES

1. Open the ASK menu and locate the TIME file. Move to the first column, if not already there, and press ⌐F6¬. A check mark appears in all other fields.

2. Open the ASK menu again and locate the EMPLOYEE file. Once again, move to the first column and press ⌐F6¬. Then, move to the Employee # column, and press ⌐F6¬ to clear the check mark in that column.

3. Combine the two files by placing an Example Element in the *Employee* # field of both databases. Rename the new file EMPTIME1.

4. Make a printout of the new file's records and its structure.

**The Structure of the New EMPTIME1 File**

This is how your file should appear after you finish Exercise 1.

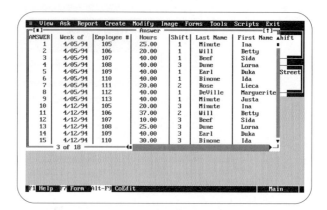

---

**EXERCISE 2**

---

## JOINING SELECTED FIELDS FROM THE EMPLOYEE AND TIME FILES

1. Open the ASK menu and locate the TIME file.

2. Open the ASK menu again and locate the EMPLOYEE file.

3. Combine the two files by placing an Example Element in the *Employee* # field of both databases but this time, only include the *Employee* #, *Last name*, *Dept*, *Hours*, and *Payrate* fields in the new file. Rename the new file EMPTIME2.

4. Make a printout of the new file's records and its structure.

**The Structure of the New EMPTIME2 File**

This is how your file should appear after you finish Exercise 2.

| 2/25/93 | | Standard Report | | | Page    1 |
|---------|-------|-----------|------|---------|------|
| Employee # | Hours | Last Name | Dept | Payrate | |
| 105 | 20.00 | Minute | 1 | 8.50 | |
| 105 | 25.00 | Minute | 1 | 8.50 | |
| 106 | 20.00 | Will | 2 | 7.00 | |
| 106 | 37.00 | Will | 2 | 7.00 | |
| 107 | 10.00 | Beef | 1 | 8.00 | |
| 107 | 40.00 | Beef | 1 | 8.00 | |
| 108 | 25.00 | Dune | 1 | 6.50 | |
| 108 | 40.00 | Dune | 1 | 6.50 | |
| 109 | 40.00 | Earl | 1 | 8.00 | |
| 110 | 30.00 | Binone | 2 | 6.75 | |
| 110 | 40.00 | Binone | 2 | 6.75 | |
| 111 | 20.00 | Rose | 1 | 8.50 | |
| 111 | 40.00 | Rose | 1 | 8.50 | |
| 112 | 40.00 | DeVille | 1 | 7.50 | |
| 113 | 40.00 | Minute | 1 | 7.00 | |

# REVIEW

- To work with two or more related files, use the ASK command and open a Query window for each file.
- To create a new file from two existing files with a common field, use the ASK command and Example Elements.

# QUESTIONS

## FILL IN THE BLANK

1. To open more than one file use the _____ command one time for each file that you want to use.
2. When linking two files, you must place Example Elements in the _____ field.
3. To link a file named TARGET to a file named SOURCE based on a field named *Common*, you would use the _____ command.
4. After two files have been combined, use the _____-_____ command sequence to change the name and create a permanent file.
5. To combine a file named SOURCE with a file named TARGET based on a field named COMMON, you would use the _____ command.

## MATCH THE COLUMNS

1. Common field
2. Example Element
3. Ctrl-R command
4. Check-marked fields

___ Rearranges fields in an Answer table
___ Assigned to common fields when linking databases
___ Used to link two or more databases
___ Only these fields are displayed

## WRITE OUT THE ANSWERS

1. Describe how you would link two files and display all of the fields from both files.
2. Describe how you would combine all of the fields in two files into one new file with the ASK command.
3. Explain what an Example Element does.
4. How do you create an Example Element?

# PROJECTS

---

## PROJECT 1

---

### RELATING THE TITLES AND SALES DATABASE FILES

1. Link the TITLES database and the SALES database based on the *ISBN* field.
2. Print a list of the linked table.

---

## PROJECT 2

---

### JOINING THE TITLES AND SALES DATABASE FILES

1. Link the TITLES database and the SALES database based on the ISBN. The new file should only contain fields that display the ISBN, title, author, period, and sales in the trade, educational, mail, and international markets.
2. Create a new file named ROYALTY.
3. Print a list of the new file.

# Printing Reports & Designing Custom Input Screens

**TOPIC 18** | *Printing Reports - Advanced Procedures*

**After completing this topic, you will be able to:**
- Arrange a report in a specific order
- Use conditions to control the records included in a report
- Modify an existing report format
- Group a report on expressions
- Print subtotals and totals
- Borrow a report format from another database family
- Temporarily change the order of records before creating a printout

When you define a report format, you control the presentation of your data. You can use keys, indexes, and filters to determine the order of the records, specify which fields or records are to be included, and specify if totals and subtotals are to be calculated.

To calculate subtotals, specify which field is to be the basis for the subtotal groupings. This field is not the field that contains the numbers, but is any field that contains duplicate data. For example, in a report that contains a field named *ST* (for state) and a field named *Amount*, specify the *ST* field to generate a report that totals (or subtotals) amounts by state.

## ▶ PARADOX TUTORIAL

In this tutorial, you will create a report form named *AMOUNTS* for the NEWFILE1 file created in Topic 17. As you do so, you will explore how to organize the data in reports and create subtotals for fields with identical entries.

**GETTING STARTED**

1. If necessary, set the default drive to drive A (or B).

**CREATING THE REPORT**

2. Open the REPORT menu, choose Design, and select NEWFILE1 from the list that appears.

■ ■ ■ ■ ■ ■ ■ ■

## ADDING A HEADING

3. Select the first Unused Report option from the list, press Enter↵ (or click OK), and type the description **AMOUNTS DUE** in the dialog box. This description will be used as a title on your finished report.

4. Press Enter↵ (or click OK).

5. When the last box appears, choose Tabular, and press Enter↵ one more time. The main Report Design screen is displayed.

**The Report Design Screen**
The Report Design screen is used to define the appearance of your finished reports.

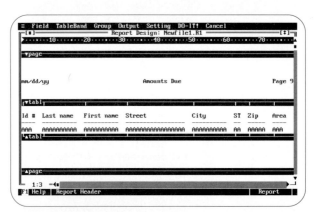

## DEFINING THE COLUMNS

6. Move the cursor to the Id # column. Open the TABLEBAND menu, select Erase, and press Enter↵. The Id # column disappears.

7. Move the cursor to the Street column. Open the TABLEBAND menu, select Erase, and press Enter↵ again. This time the Street column is erased.

8. Repeat Step 7 to erase the City, ST, Zip, Date, Age, Date-1, Remarks, Item Description, and Payment Method columns. In other words, when you are finished, you should see only the Last name, First name, Area, Phone, and Amount columns.

   If you make a mistake during this process, choose CANCEL from the menu bar and start over.

9. Move the cursor until it is below the line labeled *table* and at the bottom of the Amount column. In other words, move to the place that the new, calculated field should display.

10. Open the FIELD menu, choose Place, then Summary, and finally Regular. When the list of fields displays, choose Amount and press Enter↵ (or click OK).

11. When you see the last series of menus, choose Sum, then Overall.

12. You will see a message at the top of the screen. If necessary, move the cursor until it is where you want the new field to appear and press Enter↵.

13. The message at the top of the screen will change. Press the left arrow key seven times. When you are finished, the new field should display *99,999*. When you are ready, press Enter↵.

14. The message at the top of the screen will change one more time. If necessary, press the right arrow key until *.99* appears. If necessary, insert spaces until the right side of the new field lines up with the existing *Amount* field as shown in the illustration below. When you are finished, press Enter↵ again.

**NOTE**

Paradox will let you create new fields based on the data in existing fields. In this exercise you will create a new field at the bottom of the Amount column that will automatically sum (add) all of the numbers in that column.

**NOTE**

You may need to press Ins on the keyboard in order to insert spaces.

15. Move the cursor directly to the left of the new field and type the title **Total for amount**.

**The Finished NEWFILE1 Report**

When you are finished defining the new report for the NEWFILE1 file, your screen will look like the one shown here.

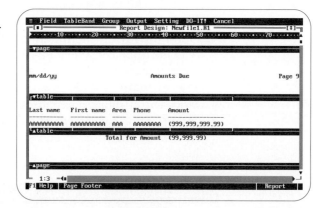

## SAVING THE REPORT FORMAT

16. When you are satisfied with the arrangement, press ⟨F2⟩ (DO-IT!).

## PREVIEWING THE REPORT

17. Open the REPORT menu and choose Output. Select NEWFILE1 from the list, then choose Amounts Due from the list of available reports.

18. When the next box appears, choose Screen. You will need to use the scroll bar on the right side of the display to see the entire report. When you finish, choose CANCEL to clear the screen.

**The NEWFILE1 Report**

When you send the NEWFILE1 report to the screen, this is what you should see.

```
2/25/93                        Amounts Due                    Page    1
Last name    First name   Area  Phone        Amount

Frog         Ura          508   555-1009         27.99
Will         Betty        203   555-1001          9.95
Will         Betty        203   555-1001         29.95
Time         Lotta        312   555-1003          9.95
Bellum       Sara         201   555-1006         13.95
Dactal       Terry        408   555-1005         57.77
Dactal       Perry        508   555-1008         39.95
Driver       Lori         201   555-1004         14.95
Driver       Lori         201   555-1004         39.95
Framed       Iben         201   555-1010          9.95
Framed       Iben         201   555-1010         59.75
Itwork       Will         407   555-1265         29.95
Burnem       Chrispin     415   555-2653         39.95
Burnem       Chrispin     415   555-2653         11.50
Burnem       Chrispin     415   555-2653         29.95
Burnem       Chrispin     415   555-2653         99.97
                     Total for Amount     525.43
```

## ARRANGING DATA BY GROUPS

19. Open the REPORT menu and choose Change. When the list appears, choose NEWFILE1.

20. When the list of available reports appears, choose Amounts Due and press ⟨Enter ←⟩. Next you will see a dialog box that displays the report title. Press ⟨Enter ←⟩ again to display the Report Design screen.

21. Use the arrow keys (or the mouse) to position the cursor in the Last name column between the horizontal lines marked *table*.

22. Open the TABLEBAND menu, choose Insert, and press ⟨Enter ←⟩. A new, blank column appears on the left side of the screen.

Ctrl-y to delete the line
ERASE

23. Use the arrow keys (or the mouse) to position the cursor so that it is just above the short vertical line that marks the left hand bottom edge of the new column. Make sure that it is above the lower horizontal line marked *table*.

24. Open the FIELD menu, choose Place, then Regular. When the list of fields appears, select Id # and press Enter ↵. If the cursor is in the correct place, press Enter ↵ again, and your new field appears. Press Enter ↵ again to make the placement "permanent."

25. Move the cursor up two lines and all the way to the left. Type **Id #**, then use the hyphen to add a divider line below the new field title. At this point, your screen should look like the illustration shown here.

**The Modified NEWFILE1 Report**
When you are finished modifying the report for NEWFILE1, your screen should look like the one shown here.

```
≡ Field  TableBand  Group  Output  Setting  DO-IT↑  Cancel
 ─[■]──────────── Report Design: Newfile1.R1 ─────────────[↕]─
 ►·······10·······20·······30·······40·······50·······60·······70·······
 ┌─▼page─
 │
 │
 mm/dd/yy                        Amounts Due                        Page 9
 │
 ┌─▼table─
 │
 Id #          Last name   First name  Area  Phone    Amount
 ─────────     ─────────   ─────────   ───   ─────    ──────
 AAA           AAAAAAAAAA  AAAAAAAAAA  AAA   AAAAAAAA (999,999,999.99)
 └─▲table─
                      Total for Amount      (99,999.99)
 ┌─▲page─
     1:3  ◄█
 F1 Help │ Table Band                                      Report
```

26. Open the GROUP menu, choose Insert, then Field, and select Id # from the list of available fields.

27. Use the arrow keys to move the cursor until it is somewhere below the Amounts Due title (at the top of the report), but above the top horizontal line marked *table*. Press Enter ↵ and a division called a *Group Band* appears.

   You will see two new horizontal divisions marked *group Id #*. They will be located above and below the division marked *table*.

28. Move the cursor until it is at the bottom of the Amount column, below the line labeled *table*, but above the new line labeled *group Id #*.

29. Open the FIELD menu, choose Place, then Summary, and finally Regular. When the list of fields displays, choose Amount, and press Enter ↵ (or click OK).

30. When you see the last series of menus, choose Sum, then PerGroup.

31. You will see a message at the top of the screen. If necessary, move the cursor until it is where you want the new field to appear and press Enter ↵.

32. The message at the top of the screen will change. Press the left arrow key seven times. When you finish, the new field should display *99,999*. When you are ready, press Enter ↵.

33. The message at the top of the screen will change one more time. If necessary, press the right arrow key until *.99* appears, then press Enter ↵ again.

34. You might want to add spaces until the right edge of the new field lines up with the existing *Amount* field as shown in the illustration

below. When you are satisfied with the arrangement, press [F2] (DO-IT!). Paradox saves the modified report.

**PRINTING THE NEW REPORT**

35. Open the REPORT menu and choose Output. Select NEWFILE1 from the list, then choose Amounts Due from the list of available reports.

36. When the next box appears, choose Printer. The records will be subtotaled and ordered according to the Id number.

**The Modified NEWFILE1 Printout**
Your final report should look similar to the one shown here.

```
2/25/93                         Amounts Due                        Page    1
Id #          Last name   First name  Area  Phone          Amount

114           Frog        Ura         508   555-1009         27.99
                                                             27.99
115           Will        Betty       203   555-1001          9.95
115           Will        Betty       203   555-1001         29.95
                                                             39.90
116           Time        Lotta       312   555-1003          9.95
                                                              9.95
117           Bellum      Sara        201   555-1006         13.95
                                                             13.95
118           Dactal      Terry       408   555-1005         57.77
                                                             57.77
119           Dactal      Perry       508   555-1008         39.95
                                                             39.95
120           Driver      Lori        201   555-1004         14.95
120           Driver      Lori        201   555-1004         39.95
                                                             54.90
121           Framed      Iben        201   555-1010          9.95
121           Framed      Iben        201   555-1010         59.75
                                                             69.70
122           Itwork      Will        407   555-1265         29.95
                                                             29.95
123           Burnem      Chrispin    415   555-2653         39.95
123           Burnem      Chrispin    415   555-2653         11.50
123           Burnem      Chrispin    415   555-2653         29.95
123           Burnem      Chrispin    415   555-2653         99.97
                                                            181.37
              Total for Amount            525.43
```

**BORROWING A REPORT FORM THAT HAS ALREADY BEEN DEFINED**

37. Open the ASK menu. When the list of files appears, choose NEWFILE1.

38. If it is not already there, move the cursor to the first field (NEWFILE1) and press [F6]. A check mark should appear in all of the other fields. Move to the *Amount* field and type **>29.00**. When you are finished, press [F2] (DO_IT!). An Answer table appears. Only the customers that spent more than $29.00 are displayed.

39. Open the TOOLS menu, select Copy, Report, and then Different Table. Press [Enter ↵] (or click OK), choose NEWFILE1 as the Source table, then select Amounts Due from the list of available reports.

40. Press [Enter ↵] again (or click OK) and choose ANSWER as the Target table. Select the first Unused Report option from the list and press [Enter ↵] (or click OK). A message appears at the bottom of the screen while Paradox copies the report from NEWFILE1 to ANSWER.

41. Open the REPORT menu and choose Output. When the list of files appears, select ANSWER. Finally, choose Amounts Due from the list of available reports and send your report to the printer.

**Using a "Borrowed" Report**

In this illustration the ANSWER table from Step 38 was printed with a report form that was "borrowed" from the NEWFILE1 database.

```
2/25/93                      Amounts Due                          Page    1
Id #          Last name   First name   Area   Phone         Amount

115           Will         Betty        203    555-1001        29.95
                                                               29.95
118           Dactal       Terry        408    555-1005        57.77
                                                               57.77
119           Dactal       Perry        508    555-1008        39.95
                                                               39.95
120           Driver       Lori         201    555-1004        39.95
                                                               39.95
121           Framed       Iben         201    555-1010        59.75
                                                               59.75
122           Itwork       Will         407    555-1265        29.95
                                                               29.95
123           Burnem       Chrispin     415    555-2653        39.95
123           Burnem       Chrispin     415    555-2653        29.95
123           Burnem       Chrispin     415    555-2653        99.97
                                                              169.87
                   Total for Amount           427.19
```

## FINISHING UP

42. You have completed this tutorial. Press [Alt]-[F8] to clear the desktop and close all open files. Go on to the next activity or exit the program.

# QUICK REFERENCE

Report formats improve the appearance of your printed data. You can print reports in a specified order, you can total and subtotal numeric fields, and you can group related records. In addition, you can save your report formats so you don't need to repeat all of the preparatory steps every time you need to print a report.

To modify an existing report format, use the REPORT-CHANGE command sequence. The menus and commands used to modify the report are the same menus and commands used to create it.

When you create (or modify) a report format, you can total (or subtotal) numeric columns. Open the FIELD menu, choose Place, and move the cursor to the correct location. Paradox can sum, average, count, and determine highest and lowest entry in a field.

You can also group related records by defining Group Bands. Open the GROUP menu, select the name of the field used as a basis for the group, and tell Paradox where to place the new band.

# EXERCISES

## EXERCISE 1

### USING THE EMPLOYEE REPORT WITH AN INDEXED FILE

1. Modify the Employee List report for the EMPLOYEE file that you created in Topic 11.
2. Group the report based on the *Department* field.
3. Print the report on your printer.

# Printing Labels

**After completing this topic, you will be able to:**
- Define, modify, and print labels

There is more than one way to print the information in your database. For example, think of all the printed labels you see every day. Letters and packages have mailing labels, items in a store's inventory have price labels, and program disks (like those used in this course) have identification labels. If you need to make a few labels, any method will suffice, but if you have to prepare thousands of labels, your computer can save an enormous amount of time.

One advantage of using a database to print labels is the flexibility that it gives you. For example, the post office offers reduced bulk rates when you presort your mail by zip code. In addition, you do not need to print all the records in your database; you can print only those that meet specific criteria.

You can easily buy labels that are gummed and mounted on sheets so that they can be run through a printer. All you need to do is pull names and other information from a database file and "fill in" these labels.

**Mailing Labels**

Mailing labels are available in a variety of formats for both dot-matrix and laser printers.

## PARADOX TUTORIAL

In this tutorial, you will create a report that prints standard 1-inch by 4-inch mailing labels using the names and addresses stored in the CUSTOMER database file.

## GETTING STARTED

1. If necessary, set the default to drive A (or B).

## CREATING A LABEL DEFINITION

2. Open the REPORT menu, choose Design, and when the file list appears, select CUSTOMER.
3. When the list of available reports displays, choose the first Unused Report option and name it *Mailing Labels*.
4. Finally, when the next selection box appears, choose Free-form. The Report Design screen is displayed.

## DEFINING THE LABEL SIZE

5. Press Ctrl-V to display the vertical ruler. You will use the vertical ruler to help you count the lines on your label.
6. If it is not already there, move the cursor up to line one and make sure that it is all the way to the left margin. Press Ctrl-Y and the first line should disappear. The horizontal dividing line (marked *page*) should now be on the first line.

   If the system beeps when you press Ctrl-Y, make sure that the cursor is all the way to the left. Remember, to delete a line the cursor must be on the left margin.

7. Move the cursor down one line until it is below the *page* divider line. Press Ctrl-Y until the divider line marked *form* is on line two. Remember, make sure that the cursor is all the way to the left.
8. Move the cursor down until it is below the divider line marked *form*. Press Ctrl-Y until there are no spaces between the *form* and *page* divider lines. When you finish, your screen should look something like the figure below.

### NOTE

Before you begin to construct your label, you must delete all of the header and footer information. When you are printing mailing labels, Paradox treats each label as if it were a single tiny page. Remember, headers print at the top of every page and footers print at the bottom. Normally, labels do not have headers and footers.

**The Free Form Report Design Screen**
You use the Free Form Report Design screen to establish the appearance of your mailing labels.

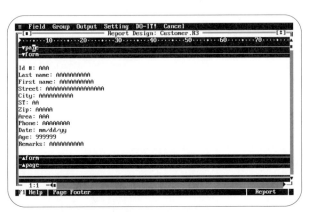

## SPECIFYING THE LABEL'S CONTENTS

9. Delete the *Id*, *ST*, *Zip*, *Area*, *Phone*, *Date*, *Age*, and *Remarks* fields. Remember, to delete a line, move the cursor to the left margin and press Ctrl-Y.
10. Move the cursor to the text that reads *Last name:*. Press the delete key until this text disappears.
11. Use Ctrl-Y to delete the line that reads *First name:*. Move the cursor up one line (to the beginning of the previous line) and press Ins.

Press the spacebar (to put a space between the fields), then move the cursor back to the left edge of the screen. Open the FIELD menu. When the pull-down menu displays, choose Place, then Regular. When the list of fields appears, choose First name, and press [Enter ↵].

The *First name* field appears and the *Last name* field moves to make space for it. Press [Enter ↵] two times to place the field.

12. Move the cursor to the line that reads *Street:* and use [Del] to erase the text there.

13. Move the cursor to the line that reads *City:* and use [Del] to delete that text. Type a comma and a space after the city field.

14. Move the cursor to the end of the city field (the end of the last line, after the comma), and open the FIELD menu. When the pull-down menu displays, choose Place, then Regular. When the list of fields appears, choose ST, and press [Enter ↵]. Press [Enter ↵] two more times to place the field.

15. Move the cursor to the end of the line again, press the spacebar, and open the FIELD menu. When the pull-down menu displays, choose Place, and then Regular one more time. This time, when the list of fields appears, choose Zip and press [Enter ↵]. Press [Enter ↵] two times to place the field.

When you finish, your screen should look like the figure below. If necessary, delete any extra lines (with [Ctrl]-[Y]) or add blank lines by pressing [Enter ↵]. Make sure that the line count (on the vertical ruler) is the same on your screen as it is here.

**The Label's Contents**
When your label is defined, the Report Design screen should look like this.

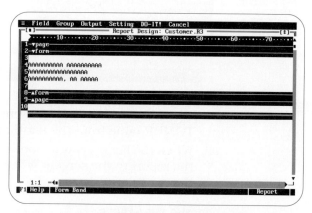

**REMOVING BLANK LINES AND EXTRA SPACES**

16. Open the SETTING menu, choose RemoveBlanks, LineSqueeze, Yes, and finally Fixed. This setting tells Paradox to use every line on a label even if it is blank.

If you do not choose this setting and one of your mailing labels only has two lines, all of the remaining labels could print on the wrong line.

17. Open the SETTING menu again and choose RemoveBlanks. This time, select FieldSqueeze, then Yes. This setting tells Paradox to remove any extra spaces in each field.

If you do not choose this setting, the first and last names will stretch across the entire line. Also, there will be additional, unwanted spaces between the city, state, and zip code on the last line of your labels. This setting gives your mailing labels a more professional appearance.

### SETTING THE PAGE WIDTH

18. Open the SETTING menu and choose Labels. When the next box appears choose Yes, and Paradox displays the message *Label status has been recorded.*

19. Open the SETTING menu again and choose PageLayout. When the next box appears, choose Width, and type **40** in the box. Press Enter ⏎ or (click OK). A vertical divider line is displayed.

### SAVING THE LABEL DEFINITION

20. Press F2 (DO-IT!) and your label definition will be saved.

### PREVIEWING THE LABELS

**Label Preview**

Always preview your labels before printing. If anything is wrong, you can make corrections and not waste any labels.

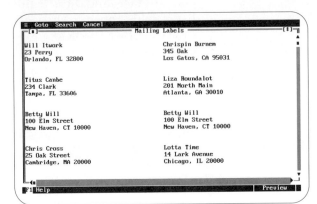

21. Open the REPORT menu, choose Output, and select the CUSTOMER table from the list that displays.

22. When the list of reports appears, choose Mailing Labels, and send the report to the screen. When you finish, select CANCEL to close the window.

### PRINTING THE LABELS

23. Open the REPORT menu, choose Output, and select the CUSTOMER table from the list that displays.

24. When the list of reports appears, choose Mailing Labels, and send the report to the printer.

**The Printed Labels**

This is how your labels will appear when they are printed on the printer.

```
Will Itwork                    Chrispin Burnem
23 Perry                       345 Oak
Orlando, FL 32800              Los Gatos, CA 95031

Titus Canbe                    Liza Roundalot
234 Clark                      201 North Main
Tampa, FL 33606                Atlanta, GA 30010

Betty Will                     Betty Will
100 Elm Street                 100 Elm Street
New Haven, CT 10000            New Haven, CT 10000

Chris Cross                    Lotta Time
25 Oak Street                  14 Lark Avenue
Cambridge, MA 20000            Chicago, IL 20000

Lori Driver                    Terry Dactal
40 Main Street                 43 Spruce Road
Edgewater, NJ 30000            Milpitas, CA 20000

Sara Bellum                    Seekum Yet
45 Porter Avenue               900 Maple Road
Fairlawn, NJ 30000             Reading, MA 20000

Perry Dactal                   Ura Frog
5 Milk Street                  5431 Washington
Salem, OR 40000                Salem, OR 40000

Iben Framed
1 Slyvan Avenue
Englewood, NJ 07632
```

## PRINTING IN INDEXED ORDER BY ZIP CODE

25. Open the REPORT menu, choose Change, and when the list of files appears, select the CUSTOMER database.

26. When the list of reports appears, select Mailing Labels. The Report Design screen is displayed.

27. Use the arrow keys to move the cursor until it is on the dividing line at the top (marked *page*). Then, open the GROUP menu, choose Insert, and then Field. When the list of fields appears, choose Zip, and press ⌊Enter←⌋ (or click OK).

28. Make sure that the cursor is on the *page* divider line (check the message at the top of the screen), and press ⌊Enter←⌋. A new divider line, marked *group zip*, appears.

29. Use the arrow keys to move the cursor to the blank line between the new group indicator and the existing *form* dividing line. Make sure that the cursor is at the left margin, press ⌊Ctrl⌋-⌊Y⌋, and the blank line disappears. Use the same procedure to delete the blank line at the bottom of your label definition.

**Printing Labels in Zip Code Order**

To print labels in zip code order, your Report Design screen should look like this.

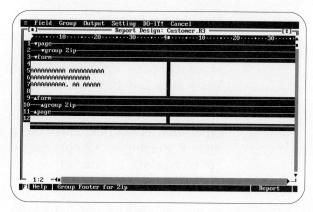

30. Press ⌊F2⌋ (DO-IT!) to save the modified label definition.

31. Open the REPORT menu, choose Output, and select the CUS-TOMER table from the list that displays.

32. When the list of reports appears, choose Mailing Labels, and send the report to the printer. This time the labels will print in zip code order.

### PRINTING SELECTED RECORDS

33. Open the ASK menu and choose CUSTOMER from the list of files that is displayed.

34. If it is not already there, use the arrow keys to move the cursor to the first column (CUSTOMER), and press [F6]. A check mark will appear in all of the other fields.

35. Move the cursor to the *State* field and type **MA**. Press [F2] (DO-IT!). A list of the selected records is displayed.

36. Open the TOOLS menu, select Copy, Report, and then DifferentTable. When the list of tables appears, choose CUSTOMER (as the Source table), and then select Mailing Labels from the list of reports.

37. When the next list of files appears, choose ANSWER (as the Target table), and select any of the Unused Report options.

38. Open the REPORT menu, choose Output, and select the ANSWER table from the list that displays.

39. When the list of reports appears, choose Mailing Labels, and send the report to the printer. Only labels for those people with *MA* in the *State* field are printed.

### FINISHING UP

40. You have completed this tutorial. Press [Alt]-[F8] to clear the desktop and close all open files. Go on to the next activity or exit the program.

## ▶ QUICK REFERENCE

When you need to print labels, you define a Free-form report. You begin by opening the REPORT menu and selecting Design. To modify an existing report, open the REPORT menu, then select Change.

### Designing Labels

Labels come in a variety of styles and sizes. For example, a common mailing label is 1-1/3 inches tall, and 4 inches wide with two labels across the page. Before you begin to lay out a report for labels, you must know how tall the labels are, how wide they are, and how many characters per inch your printer is going to print.

In general, mailing labels will be easier if you work with a fixed pitch type, such as Courier, where there are a fixed number of characters per inch. For example, 12-cpi type prints 12 characters per inch, and 10-cpi type prints 10 characters per inch. On most printers, both 10-cpi and 12-cpi will print six lines per inch down the page. If you use a proportionally spaced type, your labels may not print or align correctly because your letters may be taller or wider than you expect.

Once you know how many characters your printer prints per inch, you can begin laying out a design for labels using a grid with 10 or 12 character spaces per inch horizontally and 6 spaces per inch vertically. Alternatively, you can measure labels with a ruler and convert to characters per inch. Just multiply the measurement in inches times 10 if you are using 10-cpi type or times 12 if you are using 12-cpi type. For example, if you want a 3/4-inch left margin when using 12-cpi type, multiply .75 by 12 and you will find that the margin must be 9 characters wide.

### Eliminating Blank Spaces on Printed Labels

Frequently, you specify two or more field names on a line in a label definition. To produce labels with a more professional appearance, open the SETTING menu (while in the Report Design screen), choose RemoveBlanks, then select FieldSqueeze (or LineSqueeze).

When you specify field names in a label definition, the program automatically allocates the same number of characters on the label that are specified as the field's width. Since most fields have data shorter than the maximum field width, Paradox will print extra spaces on the label. To eliminate these spaces, use the FieldSqueeze setting. When FieldSqueeze is selected, it removes any extra blanks between fields.

If you have any records that are missing data, use the LineSqueeze setting to automatically suppress any blank lines.

### Printing Labels

Labels are printed in the same way any report is printed. Open the REPORT menu, choose the table that contains the information to be printed, choose the report format that you need to use, and send it to the printer.

When you work with a large database, you will probably want to display your labels on the screen before you start to print hundreds or even thousands of labels. To preview your results, open the REPORT menu, choose the table that contains the information to be printed, choose the report format that you need to use, and send it to the screen. When the data displays, you can use PgUp and PgDn to look at each screen page.

► E X E R C I S E S

### EXERCISE 1

### MODIFYING THE MAILING LABEL DEFINITION

Open the REPORT menu, select Change, then select the CUSTOMER database. Change the Mailing Labels report in the following ways.

a. Open the SETTING menu, select RemoveBlanks, and set FieldSqueeze to No. Print the labels.

b. Open the SETTING menu, select RemoveBlanks, and set FieldSqueeze to Yes. Remove the comma that follows the *City* field on the third line of the label, and print the labels again.

c. Move to the fourth line of the label, type **Customer ID**, add the *Id # field* to the label, and print the labels one more time.

When you have printed all three versions, compare them carefully and describe the differences.

---

## EXERCISE 2

### PRINTING LABELS FORM THE EMPLOYEE DATABASE FILE

Open the EMPLOYEE database file and define 2-across mailing labels (40 characters wide), each of which looks like the following:

```
TERRY DACTAL
400 HILL DRIVE
TAMPA, FL 33606
```

Name the form *Employee Labels* and use it to print the records in the EMPLOYEE file.

---

## EXERCISE 3

### PRINTING EMPLOYEE LABELS IN ZIP CODE ORDER

Modify the label report created in Exercise 2. Add a group band that causes the labels to print in zip code order. Print your results.

# Creating Customized Input Screens

**After completing this topic, you will be able to:**
- Use the Standard data entry form
- Create customized input screens
- Establish default values for data entry
- Control the type of data that can be entered

Up until now, you have entered data into Paradox in a form that only uses the file's field names to label the fields. If you are the only person using the database, and you know what data goes into what space, this arrangement is perfectly acceptable. However, if more than one person enters data into the same database or if you only use the file occasionally, you might want to design custom input screens.

A custom input screen might contain text that describes the type of data that can be entered, change the apparent order of the fields (to speed up data entry), or even omit certain fields to protect them from accidental changes.

You can define up to 14 custom entry screens for each database file. Paradox adds these custom forms to a table's family of files and you can use them any time you view, enter, or edit the table's data.

## ► PARADOX TUTORIAL

In this tutorial, you will select the standard form and use it to enter data for the CUSTOMER database. You will also design a custom data entry form that will be used to view, enter, and edit records in the database. The figure "The Customized Input Screen at Work" shows how the screen will look when you use it at the end of the tutorial.

**The Customized Input Screen at Work**
In this tutorial you will create a customized input screen that simplifies data entry tasks. Your screen will look like this when you are finished with the tutorial.

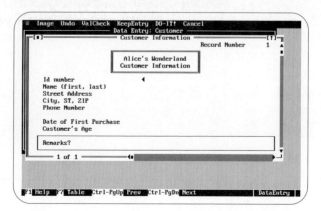

**GETTING STARTED**

1. If necessary, set the default drive to drive A (or B).

**USING THE STANDARD FORM FOR DATA ENTRY**

2. Open the MODIFY menu, select DataEntry, and when the list of files appears, choose PURCHASE.

3. Press [F7]. The Standard data entry form appears. Enter the following data and press [Enter ↵] to display a new blank form. When you have entered both records, press [F2] (DO-IT!).

| | |
|---|---|
| Id number: | 122 |
| Date: | 3/5/93 |
| Item description: | Humpty Dumpty - as is |
| Amount: | 19.95 |
| Payment method: | Check |

| | |
|---|---|
| Id number: | 121 |
| Date: | 3/17/93 |
| Item description: | Chess board |
| Amount: | 29.95 |
| Payment method: | Cash |

When you press [F2], Paradox adds the new records and displays the entire database. When you finish, press [Alt]-[F8] to close the window and clear the desktop.

**CREATING A CUSTOM DATA ENTRY SCREEN**

4. Open the FORMS menu, choose Design, and when the list of files appears, select CUSTOMER. Choose an Unused form and press [Enter ↵] or click OK. When the Form description dialog box appears, type **CUSTOMER INFORMATION** and press [Enter ↵] (or click OK).

5. Use the arrow keys to move the cursor to the row and columns as shown in the table "Literal Positions for the CUSTOMER INFORMATION Form." Type the label (shown in the table) at the cursor position. The position of the cursor is always indicated in the lower-left corner of the screen.

**NOTE**

Titles on a data entry screen that have no effect on the actual data are called *literals*. Most of the time, literals are used to create titles, describe fields, or provide prompts that help you enter data into the form correctly.

**LITERAL POSITIONS FOR THE CUSTOMER INFORMATION FORM**

| Row | Col | Label |
|---|---|---|
| 3 | 28 | Alice's Wonderland |
| 4 | 27 | Customer Information |
| 6 | 5 | Id number |
| 7 | 5 | Name (first, last) |
| 8 | 5 | Street address |
| 9 | 5 | City, ST, Zip |
| 10 | 5 | Phone number |
| 12 | 5 | Date of first purchase |
| 13 | 5 | Customer's age |
| 15 | 5 | Remarks? |

**The Completed Custom Input Screen with Literals**

When you have finished adding literals, your screen will look like this.

## FIELD POSITIONS FOR THE CUSTOMER INFORMATION FORM

| Field | Row | Col |
|-------|-----|-----|
| Id # | 6 | 30 |
| First name | 7 | 30 |
| Last name | 7 | 41 |
| Street | 8 | 30 |
| City | 9 | 30 |
| ST | 9 | 41 |
| Zip | 9 | 44 |
| Area | 10 | 30 |
| Phone | 10 | 34 |
| Date | 12 | 30 |
| Age | 13 | 30 |
| Remarks | 15 | 30 |

### PLACING THE FIELDS

6. Open the FIELD menu, select Place, then Regular. When the list of fields appears, choose the *Id #* field. Use the arrow keys to move the cursor to row 6, column 30, and then press [Enter ↵]. If everything is correct, press [Enter ↵] again to place the field in its final position.

7. Repeat this process and place the remaining fields as described in the table "Field Positions for the Customer Information Form."

### PLACING A RECORD NUMBER FIELD

When you add information to your database, Paradox automatically assigns a number to each record. Often, it is convenient if this number is displayed during data entry.

8. Use the arrow keys to move the cursor to row 1, column 50, and type **Record Number**.

9. Move the cursor to row 1, column 64. Open the FIELD menu, choose Place, and select #Record. Press [Enter ↵] twice. The record number field appears in the correct position.

### DRAWING BOXES

10. Use the arrow keys to move the cursor to row 2, column 24. Open the BORDER menu, choose Place, and select Double-line. Press [Enter ↵], and move the cursor to row 5 column 49. Press [Enter ↵] again. A double-line box appears around the title.

11. Move the cursor to row 14, column 3. Open the BORDER menu, choose Place, and select Single-line. Press [Enter ↵], and move the cursor to row 16, column 71. Press [Enter ↵] again. A single-line box appears around the Remarks area.

### ADDING COLOR TO YOUR FORM

If you do not have a color display, skip ahead to Step 17.

12. Move the cursor to row 2, column 24. Open the STYLE menu, choose Color, then choose Area. Press [Enter ↵], move the cursor to row 5, column 49, and press [Enter ↵] again.

13. When the color chart appears, press the right arrow once. The status line at the bottom of the screen should read *Blue on Cyan*, and the screen displays your color choice. Press [Enter ↵] again to select these colors.

14. Move the cursor to row 14, column 3. Open the STYLE menu, choose Color, then choose Border. Press [Enter⏎], move the cursor to row 16, column 71, and press [Enter⏎] again.

15. When the color chart appears, press the right arrow once. The status line at the bottom of the screen should read *Green on Cyan*, and the screen displays your color choice. Press [Enter⏎] again to select these colors.

16. When you have placed all of the fields and everything is arranged to your satisfaction, press [F2] to exit and save your work. The finished screen should look something like the illustration below.

**Final Screen Layout**

After entering all of the fields, labels and decorations, your customized input screen will look like this.

**NOTE**

If you find that you are entering the same data into a particular field in every record, you may want to give that field a default value. If a field has a default value, Paradox automatically fills it in for you. If the actual value of the field and the default are different, just replace the default with the correct data.

### ESTABLISHING A DEFAULT VALUE

17. Open the MODIFY menu and choose DataEntry. When the list of files appears, choose CUSTOMER.

18. When the Data Entry screen appears, open the VALCHECK menu, and choose Define. Move the cursor to the *Area* field, and press [Enter⏎]. When the menu appears, choose Default. Type **314** in the dialog box, press [Enter⏎] (or click OK), and type the following record on the first line.

| | |
|---|---|
| Id number: | 128 |
| Last name: | Deville |
| First name: | Marguerite |
| Street: | 1134 Lindenwood |
| City: | St Charles |
| State: | MO |
| Zip: | 63301 |
| Area: | (Filled in by Paradox—Press [Enter⏎]) |
| Phone: | 555-1255 |
| Date: | 4/5/93 |
| Age: | 34 |

19. Press [F2] (DO-IT!). The entire database is displayed. Paradox automatically places the new records in the correct location. When you finish, press [Alt]-[F8] to clear the desktop.

### SPECIFYING THE TYPE OF DATA THAT CAN BE ENTERED

20. Open the MODIFY menu and choose DataEntry. When the list of files appears, choose CUSTOMER.

21. When the Data Entry screen appears, open the VALCHECK menu, and choose Define. Move the cursor to the *Id* # field, and press

Enter ↵ . When the menu appears, choose Picture. Type **###** in the dialog box, and press Enter ↵ (or click OK).

22. Open the VALCHECK menu, and choose Define again. Move the cursor to the *ST* field, and press Enter ↵ . When the menu appears, choose Picture. Type **&&** in the dialog box, press Enter ↵ (or click OK), and type the following record on the first line.

| | |
|---|---|
| Id number: | 129 |
| Last name: | Beef |
| First name: | Sida |
| Street: | 136 Barnyard |
| City: | St Louis |
| State: | MO |
| Zip: | 63457 |
| Area: | (Filled in by Paradox—Press Enter ↵ ). |
| Phone: | 555-1113 |
| Date: | 4/7/93 |
| Age: | 24 |

At this point, you will not be allowed to type letters in the *Id #* field; only numbers will be accepted.

Any letters typed in the *ST* field are converted to uppercase.

23. When you finish, press F2 (DO-IT!). Paradox automatically places the new record in the correct location. When you finish, press Alt -F8 to clear the desktop.

### SPECIFYING THE FORMAT OF DATA THAT CAN BE ENTERED

24. Open the MODIFY menu and choose DataEntry. When the list of files appears, choose CUSTOMER.

25. When the Data Entry screen appears, open the VALCHECK menu, and choose Define. Move the cursor to the *Phone* field, and press Enter ↵ . When the menu appears, choose Picture. Type **###-####** in the dialog box, press Enter ↵ (or click OK), and type the following record on the first line.

| | |
|---|---|
| Id number: | 130 |
| Last name: | Saucer |
| First name: | Coopen |
| Street: | 45 Cabinet |
| City: | Redmond |
| State: | WA |
| Zip: | 90602 |
| Area: | (Filled in by Paradox—Press Enter ↵ ) |
| Phone: | 555-1123 |
| Date: | 4/7/93 |
| Age: | 27 |

Notice that when you enter the telephone number, Paradox automatically types the hyphen for you.

26. When you finish, press F2 (DO-IT!). Paradox automatically places the new record in the correct location. When you finish, press Alt -F8 to clear the desktop.

## USING THE CUSTOM INPUT SCREEN

27. Open the MODIFY menu and choose DataEntry. When the list of files appears, choose CUSTOMER.

28. When the Data Entry screen appears, open the IMAGE menu, choose PickForm, select the Customer Information form from the list, and enter the following record.

    | | |
    |---|---|
    | Id number: | 131 |
    | First name: | Bermuda (press [Enter ←] here) |
    | Last name: | Schwartz |
    | Street: | 785 North Beach |
    | City: | Orlando (press [Enter ←] here) |
    | State: | FL (press [Enter ←] here) |
    | Zip: | 10023 |
    | Area: | (Filled in by Paradox—Press [Enter ←]) |
    | Phone: | 555-1122 |
    | Date: | 4/17/93 |
    | Age: | 57 |

29. When you finish, press [F2] (DO-IT!). Paradox automatically places the new record in the correct location. When you finish, press [Alt]-[F8] to clear the desktop.

**The CUSTOMER Database**
This illustration of the CUSTOMER database shows the three new records you added.

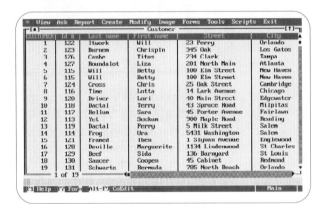

## FINISHING UP

30. You have completed this tutorial. Press [Alt]-[F8] to close all open files and clear the desktop. Go on the next activity or exit the program.

---

### ▶ Q U I C K   R E F E R E N C E

To simplify data entry, press [F7] while in the DataEntry mode, and the Standard data entry form appears. You can customize the data entry form so that it provides prompts, describes fields and displays titles to help you enter data into the form correctly.

To create a custom data entry screen, open the FORMS menu and choose Design.

#### Placing Literals

Titles on a data entry screen that have no effect on the actual data are called *literals*. Literals are used to create titles, describe fields, or provide prompts that help you enter data into the form correctly. To enter a literal, use the arrow keys to move to the correct location, and type the text.

### Placing Fields

Open the FIELD menu, select Place, then Regular. When the list appears, select the field that you want to add to the Data Entry screen. Use the arrow keys to move the cursor to the correct location, and press [Enter←]. If everything is correct, press [Enter←] again to place the field in its final position.

### Deleting Fields

If you place a field in the wrong position, or if you simply change your mind, you can delete a field by opening the FIELD menu and choosing Erase. Use the arrow keys to move to the field that you want to delete, and press [Enter←].

### Drawing Boxes

To add boxes to your data entry screen, open the BORDER menu, choose Place, and select the line type. Use the arrow keys to move to one corner of the box that you wish to draw. Press [Enter←], and move to the opposite (diagonal) corner, and press [Enter←] again.

### Using a Screen Form

Once you have designed and saved a screen definition, you can use it for data entry by opening the IMAGE menu, selecting PickForm, then selecting the form that you need from the list that appears.

## ▶ E X E R C I S E S

### EXERCISE 1

### CREATING AN INPUT SCREEN FOR THE EMPLOYEE FILE

Open the FORMS menu, select the EMPLOYEE database file, and define an input screen named *EMPLOYEE DATA* to match the one shown in the figure "The EMPLOYEE Customized Input Screen" and described in the tables "Label Positions for the EMPLOYEE Customized Input Screen" and "Field Positions for the EMPLOYEE Customized Input Screen."

### LABEL POSITIONS FOR THE EMPLOYEE CUSTOMIZED INPUT SCREEN

| Row | Col | Label |
|---|---|---|
| 2 | 29 | Employee Records |
| 4 | 5 | Employee Id number |
| 6 | 5 | Name (first, last) |
| 7 | 11 | Street |
| 8 | 7 | City, ST, Zip |
| 12 | 13 | Department |
| 13 | 15 | Payrate |

## FIELD POSITIONS FOR THE EMPLOYEE CUSTOMIZED INPUT SCREEN

| Field | Row | Col |
|---|---|---|
| Employee # | 4 | 25* |
| First name | 6 | 25 |
| Last name | 6 | 36 |
| Street | 7 | 25 |
| City | 8 | 25 |
| ST | 8 | 36 |
| Zip | 8 | 39 |
| Department | 12 | 25 |
| Payrate | 13 | 25 |

**The EMPLOYEE Customized Input Screen**
After laying out the input screen for the EMPLOYEE database file, your screen should look like this figure.

```
≡  Field  Area  Border  Page  Style  Multi  DO-IT↑  Cancel
┌[■]────────────── Form Design: Employee.F1 ─────────────[↕]─┐
│                          Employee Records                  │
│                                                            │
│         Employee Id Number  ___                            │
│                                                            │
│         Name (first, last)  _____  _____             │
│                     Street  _____                       │
│               City, ST ZIP  _____ __ ____               │
│                                                            │
│                                                            │
│                 Department  __                             │
│                   Pay rate  ____                           │
│                                                            │
│                                                            │
│                                                            │
│  15,30  1:1  ◄■                                            │
│F1 Help                                              Form   │
└────────────────────────────────────────────────────────────┘
```

## LABEL POSITIONS FOR THE TIME CUSTOMIZED INPUT SCREEN

| Row | Col | Label |
|---|---|---|
| 2 | 29 | Department records |
| 4 | 5 | Employee number |
| 6 | 7 | Week starting |
| 8 | 8 | Shift worked |
| 10 | 5 | Number of hours |

**The TIME Customized Input Screen**
After laying out the input screen for the TIME database file, your screen should look like this figure.

## FIELD POSITIONS FOR THE TIME CUSTOMIZED INPUT SCREEN

| Field | Row | Col |
|---|---|---|
| Employee # | 4 | 22 |
| Week of | 6 | 22 |
| Shift | 8 | 22 |
| Hours | 10 | 22 |

## EXERCISE 2

### CREATING AN INPUT SCREEN FOR THE TIME FILE

Open the FORMS menu, select the TIME database file, and define an input screen named *DEPARTMENT INFORMATION* to match the one shown in the figure "The TIME Customized Input Screen" and described in the tables "Label Positions for the TIME Customized Input Screen" and "Field Positions for the TIME Customized Input Screen."

**Note:** Use the arrow keys to set the *Hours* field so that it is three characters wide.

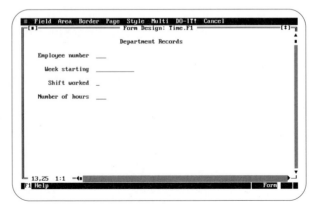

```
≡  Field  Area  Border  Page  Style  Multi  DO-IT↑  Cancel
┌[■]──────────────── Form Design: Time.F1 ───────────────[↕]─┐
│                        Department Records                  │
│                                                            │
│        Employee number  ___                                │
│                                                            │
│           Week starting  _____                          │
│                                                            │
│            Shift worked  _                                 │
│                                                            │
│         Number of hours  ___                               │
│                                                            │
│                                                            │
│  13,25  1:1  ◄■                                            │
│F1 Help                                              Form   │
└────────────────────────────────────────────────────────────┘
```

# REVIEW

- You can control the way the records appear in reports with Group Bands.
- You can modify report formats with the REPORT-CHANGE command sequence.
- You can group records in a report so that records with common entries in the same field are grouped together.
- You can have Paradox total and subtotal numeric fields in a report.
- You can define a report for mailing labels with a Free-form report.
- The LineSqueeze and FieldSqueeze commands can be used to delete blank spaces from a report.

# QUESTIONS

## FILL IN THE BLANK

1. To change the order in which records appear in a report, you specify a _____.
2. To control the records that are included in a report, you can use _____.
3. To modify a report format named MAIL, you would use the command sequence _____-_____.
4. To create a format for mailing labels, you use a _____ report format.
5. To remove trailing blanks from data, you use the _____ command.
6. To print mailing labels using an existing report, you use the _____-_____ command sequence.

## MATCH THE COLUMNS

| | |
|---|---|
| 1. REPORT-DESIGN command sequence | __ Removes blank spaces from the end of data |
| 2. Group band | __ Prints mailing labels |
| 3. REPORT-CHANGE command sequence | __ Removes blank lines from a report |
| 4. REPORT-OUTPUT command sequence | __ Designs a report format |
| 5. FieldSqueeze | __ Gathers together records with similar entries in a field |
| 6. LineSqueeze | __ Creates and revises formats for mailing labels |

## WRITE OUT THE ANSWERS

1. What command do you use to rearrange information in a report after you have created its format?
2. Describe how you would generate subtotals and totals for contributions in a report where:
   a) A field named *Member* indicates whether or not people are members.
   b) A field named *Amount* lists members' contributions.

---

**CHAPTER 6**

# PROJECTS

## PROJECT 1

### PREPARING A REPORT FOR THE ROYALTY DATABASE FILE

Prepare a report format for the ROYALTY file that lists ISBN, author, title, and period. Group the report on author names, and use the report to print the file.

# Programming with Paradox

## Creating PAL Scripts—The Basics

**After completing this topic, you will be able to:**
- Create and modify Paradox Application Language (PAL) files
- Execute and print command files

When you first use Paradox, you select commands, one at a time, from the menus at the top of your screen. However, if you find that it is necessary to enter the same series of commands over and over, you may want to store these commands in a file called a PAL script.

Technically, a PAL script is a program, and when you run a PAL script, Paradox follows the stored commands, one at a time, just as if they were entered from the keyboard. Obviously, PAL scripts can save time, and they simplify Paradox so that people with little or no experience can use the files that you have created and saved.

## ▶ PARADOX TUTORIAL

In this tutorial, you will create and execute a series of PAL scripts that illustrate the basic procedures you use to create, print, and execute Paradox command files. As you create and execute these files, you'll see how many repetitive tasks can be automated so that you can execute them with a single command. The PAL scripts you will create include the following:

- The BEGIN script introduces you to the edit screen and editing commands.
- The STARTUP script opens the MEMBERS file and displays it on your desktop.
- The SCREEN script selects a custom data entry form, then displays the CUSTOMER file for editing.
- The DISPLAY script opens the CUSTOMER file but only displays the *First name*, *Last name*, *Area*, and *Phone* fields.
- The LINKING script opens the CUSTOMER and PURCHASE files, relates them based on the Id numbers, then displays selected fields from each file.
- The QUERY script is a modification of the LINKING file that displays only purchases paid in cash.

After completing these scripts, you should have a basic understanding of Paradox command files. When entering the PAL scripts, keep the following points in mind:

■ To save time, commands are not explained each time they are used, but are described in the Quick Reference section at the end of this topic.

■ The lines in each script that begin with a semicolon are comment lines that are not executed when the command files run. They are used to document the scripts and make them easier to read. Read these lines carefully because they describe what each part of the command file is doing. However, they are not required. Your scripts will execute perfectly without them.

■ If you encounter any problems while executing your programs, refer to "Troubleshooting PAL Scripts" in the Quick Reference section.

**THE BEGIN SCRIPT**

1. If necessary, set the default drive to drive A (or B).

2. Choose SCRIPTS from the menu bar. When the pull-down menu appears, select Editor, then New. When the dialog box appears, type **BEGIN** and press Enter↵ (or click OK).

3. Enter the script shown in the figure "The BEGIN Script." Be sure to enter the two question marks and the quotation marks around the text on the four lines that begin with the @ character. Editor commands are described in the table "Editor Commands" in the Quick Reference section.

> **NOTE**
>
> Paradox automatically adds the extension .SC to the script name.

**The BEGIN.SC Script**
This is what you type to create the BEGIN script. When you play this script, it will display a message on your screen.

```
; Program Name  : BEGIN.SC  by (your name here)
; Date          : (enter today's date here)
;
; Clear the screen
CLEAR
;
; Display a message
@ 1,5 ?? "Hello, my name is (enter your name here)"
@ 2,5 ?? "(Press any key to continue)"
;
; Wait for a key to be pressed
keycode=getchar()
;
; Display another message
@ 4,5 ?? "The GETCHAR() command worked!"
@ 5,4 ?? "(Press any key to continue)"
;
; Wait for another key
keycode=getchar()
```

4. Open the FILE menu and choose Save.

5. Open the FILE menu again and choose Print. Compare the printout with the figure "The BEGIN.SC Script." If there are any differences, correct them and save your file again. When you finish, press F2 (DO-IT!) to leave the editor.

6. Open the SCRIPTS menu, and select Play. When the list of scripts appears, choose BEGIN. The text you enclosed in quotations in the lines beginning @ *1,5* and @ 2,5 appears on the screen.

   Press any key and the lines of text specified in the next series of @ commands are displayed. When you finish, press any key and the script will end.

## THE STARTUP SCRIPT

7. Choose SCRIPTS from the menu bar. When the pull-down menu appears, select Editor, then New. When the dialog box appears, type **STARTUP** and press Enter⏎ (or click OK).

8. Enter the file shown in the figure "The STARTUP.SC Script."

**The STARTUP.SC Script**
Here is the contents of the STARTUP script. It will automatically load the CUSTOMER database file.

```
; Program name : STARTUP.SC by (enter your name here)
; Date         ; (enter today's date here)
;
; Clear the screen
clear
;
; Open the CUSTOMER database file
VIEW "Customer"
```

9. Open the FILE menu and choose Save.

10. Open the FILE menu again and choose Print. Compare the printout with the figure "The STARTUP.SC Script." If there are any differences, correct them and save your file again. When you finish, press F2 (DO-IT!) to leave the editor.

11. Open the SCRIPTS menu, and select Play. When the list of scripts appears, choose STARTUP. The CUSTOMER table is displayed.

12. When you finish, press Alt-F8 to close the window and clear the desktop.

## THE SCREEN SCRIPT

13. Choose SCRIPTS from the menu bar. When the pull-down menu appears, select Editor, then New. When the dialog box appears, type **SCREEN** and press Enter⏎ (or click OK).

14. Enter the file shown in the figure "The SCREEN.SC Script."

**The SCREEN.SC Script**
This script will load the CUSTOMER database and select the CUSTOMER INFORMATION custom display screen.

```
; Program name : SCREEN.SC by (enter your name here)
; Date         ; (enter today's date here)
;
; Clear the screen
clear
; Load the CUSTOMER database
VIEW "customer"
; Load the custom data entry form
Pickform 1
```

15. Open the FILE menu and choose Save.

16. Open the FILE menu again and choose Print. Compare the printout with the figure "The SCREEN.SC Script." If there are any differ-

ences, correct them and save your file again. When you finish, press F2 (DO-IT!) to leave the editor.

17. Open the SCRIPTS menu, and select Play. When the list of scripts appears, choose SCREEN. The script displays the CUSTOMER file using the customized input screen named *CUSTOMER INFORMATION*. Use PgUp and PgDn to move through the records.

18. When you finish, press Alt-F8 to close the window and clear the desktop.

### THE DISPLAY SCRIPT

19. Choose SCRIPTS from the menu bar. When the pull-down menu appears, select Editor, then New. When the dialog box appears, type **DISPLAY** and press Enter← (or click OK).

20. Enter the file shown in the figure "The DISPLAY.SC Script."

**The DISPLAY.SC Script**
When you play this script, Paradox will load a predefined query named *ANSWERS*, and apply that query to the CUSTOMERS database file.

```
; Program name : DISPLAY.SC by (enter your name here)
; Date         : (enter today's date here)
;
; Clear the screen
Clear
;
; Load and use the saved query named ANSWERS
; Note: In the next line, be sure to include the quotes
Play "answers"
;
; Display the answer table
DO_IT!
```

21. Open the FILE menu and choose Save.

22. Open the FILE menu again and choose Print. Compare the printout with the figure "The DISPLAY.SC Script." If there are any differences, correct them and save your file again. When you finish, press F2 (DO-IT!) to leave the editor.

23. Open the ASK menu. When the list of files appears, choose CUSTOMER. Place a check mark in the *Last name*, *First name*, *Area* and *Phone* fields. Remember, to place a check mark, use the arrow keys to move the cursor into the correct field and press F6.

24. Open the SCRIPTS menu and select QuerySave. When the dialog box appears, type **ANSWERS** and press Enter← (or click OK).

25. Press Alt-F8 to close the Query window and clear the desktop.

26. Open the SCRIPTS menu, and select Play. When the list of scripts appears, choose DISPLAY. The CUSTOMER database is displayed, but only the fields that you selected in the Query window are visible.

27. When you finish, press Alt-F8 to close the window and clear the desktop.

### THE LINKING SCRIPT

28. Choose SCRIPTS from the menu bar. When the pull-down menu appears, select Editor, then New. When the dialog box appears, type **LINKING** and press Enter← (or click OK).

29. Enter the file shown in the figure "The LINKING.SC Script."

**The LINKING.SC Script**

When you play this script, Paradox will load a predefined query named *ANSWERS*, and apply that query to the CUSTOMERS database file.

```
; Program Name : LINKING.SC (enter your name here)
; Date         ; (enter today's date here)
;
; Clear the screen
Clear
;
; Load and use the saved query named LINKANS
; Don't forget to use the quotes in the next statement
PLAY "linkans"
;
; Display the answer table
DO_IT!
```

30. Open the FILE menu and choose Save.

31. Open the FILE menu again and choose Print. Compare the printout with the figure "The LINKING.SC Script." If there are any differences, correct them and save your file again. When you finish, press [F2] (DO-IT!) to leave the editor.

32. Open the ASK menu. When the list of files appears, choose CUSTOMER. Place a check mark in the *Last name* and *First name* fields.

33. Move the cursor to the *Id #* field in the CUSTOMER window and enter the Example Element **NUMBER**. Remember, to place an Example Element, press [F5], then type the name.

34. Open the ASK menu again. When the list of files appears, choose PURCHASE. Place a check mark in the *Amount* and *Payment Method* fields.

35. Move the cursor to the *Id #* field in the PURCHASE window and enter the Example Element **NUMBER**.

36. Open the SCRIPTS menu and select QuerySave. When the dialog box appears, type **LINKANS** and press [Enter ←] (or click OK).

37. Press [Alt]-[F8] to close the Query window and clear the desktop.

38. Open the SCRIPTS menu, and select Play. When the list of scripts appears, choose LINKING. After a few seconds, an Answer table will open. It displays the *First name* and *Last name* fields from the CUSTOMER database and the *Amount* and *Payment Method* fields from the PURCHASE database.

39. When you finish, press [Alt]-[F8] to close the Answer table and clear the desktop.

**MODIFYING THE LINKING SCRIPT**

40. Open the ASK menu. When the list of files appears, choose CUSTOMER. Place a check mark in the *Last name* and *First name* fields.

41. Move the cursor to the *Id #* field in the CUSTOMER window and enter the Example Element **NUMBER**.

42. Open the ASK menu again. When the list of files appears, choose PURCHASE. Place a check mark in the *Amount* and *Payment Method* fields.

43. Move the cursor to the *Id #* field in the PURCHASE window and enter the Example Element **NUMBER**.

44. Move the cursor to the *Payment Method* field and type **Cash** (remember to watch upper and lower case).

45. Open the SCRIPTS menu and select QuerySave. When the dialog box appears, type **LINKANS** and press [Enter ⏎] (or click OK). When the confirmation box appears, choose Replace.

46. Press [Alt]-[F8] to close the Query window and clear the desktop.

47. Open the SCRIPTS menu, and select Play. When the list of scripts appears, choose LINKING. After a few seconds an Answer table will open. It displays the *First name* and *Last name* fields from the CUSTOMER database and the *Amount* and *Payment Method* fields from the PURCHASE database, but only the if the word *Cash* appears in the *Payment Method* field.

48. When you finish, press [Alt]-[F8] to close the Answer table and clear the desktop.

**FINISHING UP**

49. You have completed this tutorial. If necessary, press [Alt]-[F8] to close all open files and to clear the desktop. Go on to the next activity or exit the program.

---

## ▶ Q U I C K   R E F E R E N C E

To write or edit a PAL script file, open the SCRIPTS menu, select Editor, then New (or Open). The Paradox *editor* is displayed. The editor is much like a word processing program. You can type and edit commands, then save them on a disk. For example, to edit a script file named MENU, you would use the command sequence SCRIPTS-EDITOR-OPEN, and select the MENU file from the displayed list. If the file exists and is on the default drive, it will load into the editor and display on the screen. You do not have to specify an extension for the command file's name because Paradox automatically adds the extension *.SC* to all script files.

### EDITOR COMMANDS

| To | Press |
|---|---|
| **Cursor Movement Commands** | |
| Move cursor one character left or right | [←] or [→] |
| Move cursor to beginning or end of line | [Home] or [End] |
| Move cursor one word left or right | [Ctrl]-[←] or [Ctrl]-[→] |
| Move cursor up or down one line | [↑] or [↓] |
| Page up or down | [PgUp] or [PgDn] |
| Find text | **Search, Find** |
| Repeat previous Find command | **Search, Next** |
| **Editing Commands** | |
| Delete character | [Del] or [← Bksp] |
| Turn insert mode on and off | [Ins] |

### Save and Retrieve Commands

| | |
|---|---|
| Save file | **File, Save** |
| Abandon file without saving changes | **Cancel** |
| Copy a file on disk into file on screen at cursor's position | **File, InsertFile** |
| Copy file on screen into a file on disk | **File, CopyToFile** |
| Copy selected text to a file on disk | **File, WriteBlock** |

## Printing Script Files

You can print the contents of a script file by loading it into the editor, opening the FILE menu, and choosing Print.

## Playing Script Files

After writing or editing a script file you execute it with the SCRIPTS-PLAY command sequence. For example, to execute a command file named MENU, open the SCRIPTS menu, and select Play. When the list of fields appears, choose MENU. The commands stored in the script file are automatically executed.

## Understanding the Commands Used in the Programs in This Topic

Here are brief descriptions of each of the commands introduced in the programs in this topic.

- **@ row n, col n ??** displays text on the screen in the position specified. The text to be displayed must be enclosed in double quotation marks. For example, the command @ 1,0 ?? "Hello" displays the word *Hello* on the screen beginning in row 1, column 0. Rows are counted from top to bottom beginning with row 0. Columns are counted from left to right beginning with column 0.
- **CLEAR** clears all data from the screen.
- **Keycode=GETCHAR()** pauses the program. When you press a key, the script file goes on to the next step.
- **VIEW "Table name"** displays the contents of the specified database file exactly as if it were chosen with the VIEW menu from the main Paradox screen. For example, to view the data in a file named BOOKLIST, use the command **VIEW "BOOKLIST"**. Remember, the name of the file must be enclosed in quotations.
- **PICKFORM #** chooses a pre-defined custom display form from the list of forms. PICKFORM 1 chooses the first form from the list, PICKFORM 2 chooses the second, and so on. PICKFORM "F" chooses the standard data entry form.
- **PLAY "QueryImage name"** displays an answer table based on the image saved with the SCRIPTS-QUERYSAVE command sequence. Remember, the name of the query image must be enclosed in quotations.
- **DO_IT!** is the same as selecting DO_IT! from the main menu or pressing the [F2] key.

## Troubleshooting PAL Scripts

Most of the problems that you will encounter in a Paradox script will fall into one of the following categories.

- A *Syntax error* indicates that some part of your command is not written correctly or a word in a command is not spelled correctly. For example, if you enter *EVIW "ZIPCODE"* instead of *VIEW "ZIPCODE"*, a syntax error will occur. Check your program carefully. Look for misspellings or other typing errors.
- *Run errors* occur if a command is constructed correctly but used incorrectly. An example of a run error is a variable used in a command before it has a value or trying to use a command in the wrong mode.
- A *Logic error* is created when you use the wrong variable or file name or perform a series of operations in the wrong order. For example, the command *VIEW "ZIPCODE"* is a valid command, but if ZIPCODE does not exist, a logic error will occur.

Paradox provides a tool called the DEBUGGER that will often activate automatically whenever an error occurs. A complete discussion of the DEBUGGER is beyond the scope of this tutorial, but if an error occurs, a box will appear in the middle of your screen that says *Cancel* and *Debug*. If you select Debug, the system will display a line number and the contents of the line that seems to contain an error. To continue, press Ctrl-Q, load your script back into the editor, make any necessary corrections, and play your script again.

# ▶ E X E R C I S E S

## EXERCISE 1

### CREATING AN EMPLOYEE SCRIPT FILE

Write a PAL file that opens the EMPLOYEE database file and displays the *First name*, *Last name* and *Payrate* fields. Print out a copy of the program. **Hint:** This exercise is similar to the STARTUP script.

## EXERCISE 2

### CREATING A TIME SCRIPT FILE

Write a PAL file that displays the *First name* and *Last name* fields from the EMPLOYEE field and the *Shift* field from the TIME field. Remember to create (and save) a query before you run your script. Print out a copy of the program. **Hint:** This exercise is similar to the DISPLAY and LINKING scripts.

# Creating PAL Script Files—Advanced Procedures

**After completing this topic, you will be able to:**
- Use WHILE-ENDWHILE commands to create loops in your script files
- Use IF-ENDIF commands to branch programs based on conditions
- Display text to create menus
- Use SWITCH-CASE-ENDSWITCH commands to branch programs based on user selections

Script files can do more than just store executable commands. They can also contain "decisions" that tell your script to take a specific action based on user input or on the outcome of prior script actions. For example, a PAL script can repeat the same process again and again (called a LOOP), or perform one action if a condition is true and another if a condition is false (called a BRANCH). These capabilities make a script extremely flexible. A knowledgeable user (like you) can program it to perform almost any task.

## ▶ P A R A D O X    T U T O R I A L

In this tutorial, you will create and execute a series of programs that illustrate many features of Paradox script files.

- The LOOPING script file displays a series of numbers on the screen. The purpose of this script is to introduce you to the WHILE-ENDWHILE command and variables.
- The CHARGEN script file displays the 254 characters in the IBM PC's character set. This script is an application of the principles you first explored in LOOPING.
- The COMPRESS script file lets you set some printers to compressed or normal type. The numbers 15 and 18 in the PRINT commands are the setup codes that turn on compressed or normal type on your printer. These codes may not work with your printer but your instructor may be able to suggest alternative codes.
- MENU displays a menu on the screen so that you can make choices to add records or to view the records in the CUSTOMER and PURCHASE database files.

After completing these files, you should have a basic understanding of PAL script files. When entering the script files, keep the following points in mind:

- To save time in these tutorials, commands are not explained each time they are used, but the commands introduced in this topic are described in the Quick Reference section at the end of this topic.
- You will notice that some lines are indented. (To indent a line, press [Tab⇆] or use the spacebar.) The indents are not required, but they make the script file easier to read.

### THE LOOPING SCRIPT FILE

1. If necessary, set the default drive to drive A (or B).
2. Choose SCRIPTS from the menu bar. When the pull-down menu appears, select Editor, then New. When the dialog box appears, type **LOOPING** and press [Enter ←] (or click OK).
3. Enter the script file shown in the figure "The LOOPING.SC Script."

**The LOOPING.SC Script**

This is the contents of the LOOPING script file.

```
; Program name : LOOPING.SC by (enter your name here)
; Date         : (enter today's date here)
;
; Clear the screen
CLEAR
;
; Place a value of one in a variable named COUNTER
COUNTER = 1
;
; Mark the begining of the actual loop and define the
; conditions for its operation
WHILE COUNTER <=100
        ; Display the current value of the number in COUNTER and a blank
        ; space. (One question mark lists numbers vertically and two
        ; question marks lists them across the screen and down).
        ; Note: Type a single space between the two quote marks
        ;
        ?? COUNTER
        ?? " "
        ;
        ; Increment the number in COUNTER by 1
        COUNTER = COUNTER + 1
; Mark the end of the loop
ENDWHILE
;
;Display a closing message. Note: Only use one question mark this time.
? "I've counted as high as you asked."
;
; Wait for a key to be pressed
keycode=GETCHAR()
```

4. Open the FILE menu and choose Save.
5. Open the FILE menu again and choose Print. Compare the printout with the figure "The LOOPING.SC Script." If there are any differences, correct them and save your file again. When you finish, press [F2] (DO-IT!) to leave the editor.
6. Open the SCRIPTS menu, and select Play. When the list of scripts appears, choose LOOPING. The script file lists the numbers on the screen starting at 1. When it reaches 100, it displays the message *I've counted as high as you asked.* When you are finished, press [Esc].

**The LOOPING.SC Script When Played**

When you play the LOOPING script, your screen should look something like this.

```
1 2 3 4 5 6 7 8 9 10 11 12 13 14 15 16 17 18 19 20 21 22 23 24 25 26 27 28 29 30
 31 32 33 34 35 36 37 38 39 40 41 42 43 44 45 46 47 48 49 50 51 52 53 54 55 56 5
7 58 59 60 61 62 63 64 65 66 67 68 69 70 71 72 73 74 75 76 77 78 79 80 81 82 83
84 85 86 87 88 89 90 91 92 93 94 95 96 97 98 99 100
I've counted as high as you asked.
```

7. Choose SCRIPTS from the menu bar. When the pull-down menu appears, select Editor, then Open. When the list of files appears, choose LOOPING and press Enter↵ (or click OK). Change the number in the line *WHILE COUNTER <= 100* to **200** and press F2 (DO_IT!) to save the change.

8. Open the SCRIPTS menu, and select Play. When the list of scripts appears, choose LOOPING.

   The script file now lists the numbers 1 through 200 on the screen and then displays the message *I've counted as high as you asked.* When you are finished, press Esc.

## THE CHARGEN SCRIPT FILE

9. Choose SCRIPTS from the menu bar. When the pull-down menu appears, select Editor, then New. When the dialog box appears, type **CHARGEN** and press Enter↵ (or click OK).

10. Enter the script file shown in the figure "The CHARGEN.SC Script."

**The CHARGEN.SC Script**

This is the contents of the CHARGEN script file.

```
; Program name : CHARGEN.SC by (enter your name here)
; Date          ; (enter today's date here)
;
; Clear the screen
CLEAR
;
; Set up variables to store the ROW and COLUMN positions
atrow = 1
atcol = 4
;
   ; Set variable for COUNTER to 1
   counter = 1
   ;
   ; Start a loop that counts to 255
   WHILE counter <=255
         ; Start a loop to create rows
         WHILE atcol <=72 AND counter <=255
               @ atrow, atcol ?? STRVAL(counter) + "=" + CHR (counter)
               atcol=atcol + 6
               counter =counter + 1
         ; End loop that creates rows
         ENDWHILE
         ;
         ; Set the variables for the next row.
         atrow = atrow + 1
         atcol = 4
   ; End the loop that counts to 255
   ENDWHILE
   ;
   ; Wait for a key to be pressed
   keycode = GETCHAR()
```

11. Open the FILE menu and choose Save.

12. Open the FILE menu again and choose Print. Compare the printout with the figure "The CHARGEN.SC Script." If there are any differences, correct them and save your file again. When you finish, press [F2] (DO-IT!) to leave the editor.

13. Open the SCRIPTS menu, and select Play. When the list of scripts appears, choose CHARGEN. It will display a table of the 254 characters in the IBM PC character set. When you are finished, press [Esc].

**The CHARGEN.SC Script When Played**

When you play the CHARGEN script, your screen should display the 254 characters in the IBM PC Character set.

## THE COMPRESS SCRIPT FILE

14. Choose SCRIPTS from the menu bar. When the pull-down menu appears, select Editor, then New. When the dialog box appears, type **COMPRESS** and press [Enter←] (or click OK).

15. Enter the script file shown in the figure "The COMPRESS.SC Script."

**The COMPRESS.SC Script File**

This is the contents of the COMPRESS script file. When you play this script it will set an Epson Dot Matrix printer to compressed print. If you are not using an Epson printer, your instructor may be able to supply code that will work with your printer.

```
; Program name : COMPRESS.SC (enter your name here)
; Date         : (enter today's date here)
;
CLEAR
;
; Display a prompt and store the user's answer in a variable
@ 4,5 ?? "Print in compressed type? (Y/N)"
keycode = GETCHAR()
;
; Note: The codes used here are for an Epson dot matrix printer
;
; Start of IF statement
IF keycode = ASC("Y") or keycode = ASC("y")
        ; Do this if the user presses and upper or lower case "Y"
        ; Select the default printer
        THEN SETPRINTER "LPT1"
                ; Set printer to compressed type
                ; Note: Use a BACKSLASH here
                PRINTER ON
                ?? "\015"
                PRINTER OFF
        ; Do this if the user presses anything else.
        ; Select default printer
        ELSE SETPRINTER "LPT1"
                ; Set printer to standar type
                ; Note: Use a BACKSLASH here
                PRINTER ON
                ?? "\018"
                PRINTER OFF
; End of IF statement
ENDIF
```

16. Open the FILE menu and choose Save.

17. Open the FILE menu again and choose Print. Compare the printout with the figure "The COMPRESS.SC Script." If there are any differences, correct them and save your file again. When you finish, press F2 (DO-IT!) to leave the editor.

18. Open the SCRIPTS menu, and select Play. When the list of scripts appears, choose COMPRESS. The script file runs and displays the prompt *Print in compressed type? (Y/N)*.

19. Press Y, then Enter↵ to end the script.

20. Open the REPORT menu, and select Output. When the list of files appears, choose CUSTOMER.

21. When the selection list appears, choose Standard Report, then Printer to print the file in compressed type.

## THE MENU SCRIPT FILE

22. Choose SCRIPTS from the menu bar. When the pull-down menu appears, select Editor, then New. When the dialog box appears, type **MENU** and press Enter↵ (or click OK).

23. Enter the script file shown in the figure "The MENU.SC Script."

   ■ To align the menu that begins under the TEXT command, press Tab⇆ as necessary, then enter the text. To enter the ruled lines in the menu, use the equal sign (=).

   ■ Enter single spaces between characters and three spaces between words in the menu's title. Press Spacebar or Del as necessary to center the title horizontally in the space between the ruled line.

   ■ Sixteen spaces follow the opening quotation mark in the line *??" Enter choice, press Enter: "*. This aligns the prompt under the menu.

   ■ In this script, the comments are often placed at the end of the command line. To add a comment at the end of a line, simply type a semicolon, followed by your comment.

**The MENU.SC Script**

This is the contents of the MENU script file.

```
; Program name : MENU.SC by (enter your name here)
; Date         : (enter today's date here)
;
; Hint: Save your work frequently in case you make an error
;
; Set up main loop
WHILE (true)
        ; Display menu text
        CLEAR
        ; Move to start position for menu
        ; This time, no space between the quotes
        @ 3,0 ?? ""
        TEXT
                ============================================
                               M A I N     M E N U
                ============================================

                1.    Add names to CUSTOMER file

                2.    VIEW the CUSTOMER file

                3.    Add information to the PURCHASE file

                4.    View the PURCHASE file

                5.    Exit and return to PARADOX


                ============================================
        ENDTEXT
        ;
        ; Get input from user
        ?? "                    Please enter your choice:"
        keycode = GETCHAR()
        ;
        ; Set up beginning of tests
        SWITCH
                ; Be sure to include the colon (:) at the end
                ; of each CASE statement
                CASE keycode = ASC ("1") :
                        EDIT "CUSTOMER"      ;Open the CUSTOMER file
                        END                  ;Move to the last record
                        DOWN                 ;Move to a new, blank record
                        PICKFORM "1"         ;Select the custom entry screen
                        WAIT RECORD          ;Limit user to current record
                        PROMPT "Press [F2] when you are finished"
                        UNTIL "DO_IT!"
                        DO_IT!               ;Save record and return to menu
                        CLEARALL             ;Clear the desktop
                CASE keycode = ASC ("2") :
                        VIEW "CUSTOMER"      ;Open the CUSTOMER file
                        WAIT TABLE           ;limit user to current table
                        PROMPT "Press [F2] when you are finished"
                        UNTIL "DO_IT!"
                        DO_IT!               ;Save record and return to menu
                        CLEARALL             ;Clear the desktop
                CASE keycode = ASC ("3") :
                        EDIT "PURCHASE"      ;Open the PURCHASE file
                        END                  ;Move to the last record
                        DOWN                 ;Move to a new, blank record
                        PICKFORM "F"         ;Select standard entry screen
                        WAIT RECORD          ;Limit user to current record
                        PROMPT "Press [F2] when you are finished"
                        UNTIL "DO_IT!"
                        DO_IT!               ;Save record and return to menu
                        CLEARALL             ;Clear the desktop
                CASE keycode = ASC ("4") :
                        VIEW "PURCHASE"      ;Open the PURCHASE file
                        WAIT TABLE           ;Limit user to current table
                        PROMPT "Press [F2] when you are finished"
                        UNTIL "DO_IT!"
                        DO_IT!               ;Save record and return to menu
                        CLEARALL             ;Clear the desktop
                CASE keycode = ASC ("5") :
                        QUITLOOP             ;Exit the menu
        OTHERWISE:
                ;You only get here if the user did not enter 1 through 5
                CLEAR
                @ 8,24 ?? "You must enter 1 through 5!"
                @ 10,26 ?? "****** Try again ******"
                ; Wait 3 seconds
                SLEEP 3000
                CLEAR
        ; End of tests
        ENDSWITCH
; End of main loop
ENDWHILE
```

24. Open the FILE menu and choose Save.

25. Open the FILE menu again and choose Print. Compare the printout with the figure "The MENU.SC Script." If there are any differences, correct them and save your file again. When you finish, press [F2] (DO-IT!) to leave the editor.

26. Open the SCRIPTS menu, and select Play. When the list of scripts appears, choose MENU. Your menu appears and a flashing cursor displays on the line that reads *Please enter your choice*.

**The MENU.SC Script When Played**
When you play the MENU script, this menu is displayed on your screen.

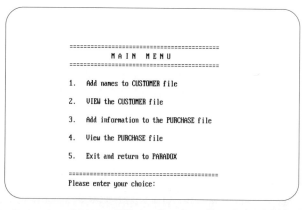

```
=================================================
                    M A I N   M E N U
=================================================

   1.    Add names to CUSTOMER file

   2.    VIEW the CUSTOMER file

   3.    Add information to the PURCHASE file

   4.    View the PURCHASE file

   5.    Exit and return to PARADOX


=================================================
Please enter your choice:
```

27. Press [1] to display a new, blank record for the CUSTOMER file.

28. Select [F2] (DO_IT!) to return to the menu.

29. Continue making choices. Press [F2] to return to the menu.

30. Try pressing any key other than 1 through 5 and watch what happens.

31. When finished, press [5] (for *Exit*) to end the script.

**FINISHING UP**

32. You have completed this tutorial. Press [Alt]-[F8] to close all open files and to clear the desktop. Go on to the next activity or exit the program.

---

## ▶ QUICK REFERENCE

To write powerful programs, you need to understand the concepts behind variables and WHILE, IF, and SWITCH commands.

### Variables

A *variable* is a storage place used like a little mailbox to store data temporarily. After naming a variable, you give it a value, and the variable can be used whenever it is needed. The value of a variable can change but the name does not. For example, the command COUNTER=1 stores the value 1 in a variable named *COUNTER*, but later you could use a statement that says *COUNTER=5*.

To see the contents of memory variables, you can place a statement in your PAL script that includes a question mark followed by the name of the variable. For example, to see the contents of the variable COUNTER, type **? COUNTER.**

A variable name must begin with a letter, cannot contain any spaces, and can be up to 132 characters long.

## WHILE-ENDWHILE Commands

Often, you will need to repeat a series of commands again and again until a certain condition is met. It's like telling someone to "empty all those boxes and put their contents on the shelves until there are no more boxes to empty." In Paradox, you structure a command of this type like this:

WHILE *<condition>*
*<commands>*
ENDWHILE

First, Paradox tests to see if the condition is true. If it is, the commands that follow are executed. When it reaches ENDWHILE, it jumps back up to the WHILE line and checks to see if the condition is still true. If it is, the program executes the commands again. It continues looping until the condition no longer evaluates as true. Then Paradox jumps to the command that follows the ENDWHILE statement.

In the LOOPING script file, the program creates a variable named *COUNTER*, and stores the number 1 in it. The WHILE statement then checks the number to see if it is less than or equal to 100. If it is, the program displays the number (?? COUNTER), then adds 1 to the number in the variable (COUNTER = COUNTER+1). The program then loops back to the WHILE line and reads the variable again. (This time it is 2.) If it is still less than or equal to 100, the commands repeat. Eventually, the variable reaches 101 and the condition is false, so the script jumps to whatever command follows the ENDWHILE line.

```
COUNTER = 0
WHILE COUNTER <= 100
?? COUNTER
COUNTER = COUNTER + 1
ENDWHILE
```

## IF Commands

In real life, you make true/false decisions every day. For example, if a rich relative were to say, "If you get an A in this course, I'll buy you a convertible; if you don't, you agree to stay in your room all next semester and study day and night." Such a statement basically says, "If this condition is met, then do one thing; if it is not met, do another."

When you write your Paradox scripts, you will encounter situations in which you want a program to branch in one direction if a condition is true or in another if it is false. In these situations, you can use an IF command. In Paradox, this kind of command is structured as:

**IF** you get an A in this course
I'll buy you a convertible
**ELSE**
You'll stay in your room and study all semester
**ENDIF**

Or, in more schematic form:

IF *<condition>*
*<commands>*

```
ELSE
<commands>
ENDIF
```

In the COMPRESS script, the user's input from the KEYCODE=GETCHAR() statement is stored in a variable named *KEYCODE*, and then evaluated by the IF statement. If the response is an uppercase or lowercase Y, then the "\015" code is sent to the printer. [ASC("Y") is a Paradox function that converts the character in the parentheses to a form that Paradox can use.] If the response isn't "Y" or "y", then the "\018" code is sent.

```
@4,5  "Print in compressed type? (Y/N) "
        keycode=GETCHAR()
IF keycode=ASC("Y") OR keycode=ASC("y")
        THEN SETPRINTER "LPT1"
        PRINTER ON
        ?? "\015"
        PRINTER OFF
ELSE SETPRINTER "LPT1"
        PRINTER ON
        ?? "\018"
        PRINTER OFF
ENDIF
```

The ELSE part of the IF command is often optional. For example, if you eliminate it and the condition in the IF command evaluates to false, the program jumps to the first command that follows the ENDIF command.

### CASE Commands

SWITCH-CASE commands are similar to IF commands, but are easier to use when there is more than one possible response. In the simplest form, this command can be set up to do the same thing the IF command does. For example:

```
SWITCH
        CASE <condition>
                <commands>
        OTHERWISE
                <commands>
ENDSWITCH
```

In this example, if CASE evaluates as true, the commands that follow are executed. If it evaluates as false, the commands after the OTHERWISE statement are executed.

Usually, the command is set up like the one in the MENU script file. There are five possible correct choices numbered 1 through 5. Each of these is listed as a CASE and each contains a separate set of commands. If any input other than a correct one is made, the commands that follow the OTHERWISE statement are executed.

```
SWITCH
        CASE keycode=ASC("1")
                EDIT "CUSTOMER"
                (other commands)
        CASE keycode=ASC("2")
```

```
                    VIEW "CUSTOMER"
                    (other commands)
        CASE keycode=ASC("3")
                    EDIT "PURCHASE"
                    (other commands)
        CASE keycode=ASC("4")
                    VIEW "PURCHASE"
                    (other commands)
        CASE keycode=ASC("5")
                    QUITLOOP
        OTHERWISE
                    @   8,24 ?? "You must enter 1 through 5!"
                    @ 10,26 ?? "****** Try Again ******"
                    SLEEP 3000
    ENDSWITCH
```

## Understanding the Commands Used in the Programs in This Topic

Here are brief descriptions of each of the commands introduced in the programs in this topic.

- **?** and **??** display or print an expression list. A double question mark starts at the current cursor position and displays each item (with no spaces between them) until the line is full. A single question mark starts at the beginning of the line below the current cursor position and displays each item (with no spaces between them) until the line is full.

- **ASC(char)** converts the specified character or key code to its ASCII value. ASC() returns a positive value if "char" is an ASCII code and returns a negative value if "char" is an IBM extended code. For example, the command **c=ASC("1")** sets the variable "c" to a value of 49 and the command **c=ASC("F10")** returns a value of -68.

- **CHR(number)** converts an ASCII value to a printable character. This command is often used to convert the results of a calculation to a form that can be printed or displayed easily.

- **CLEAR** clears all of the current PAL canvas. In other words, this command can be used to clear the display screen.

- **CLEARALL** removes all image windows from the Paradox work area. This command is the same as [Alt]-[F8] from the keyboard.

- **DO_IT!** is the same as [F2] **(DO_IT!)** from the keyboard.

- **GETCHAR()** reads a character from the keyboard and stores it in a specified variable. For example, **keypress=GETCHAR()** accepts a keystroke from the keyboard and stores it in a variable named "keypress."

- **IF-ELSE-ENDIF** performs one of two command sequences based on the evaluation of a logical condition. If the condition that follows an IF statement is true, then the commands that immediately follow are executed. If the condition is false, the commands that follow the ELSE statement are executed.

- **PRINTER ON** is used to send all of the output that follows to the selected printer. When the printing is complete, use the command **PRINTER OFF**.

- **SETPRINTER** selects one of the printers connected to your computer system. The primary printer is usually named *LPT1* so this command will often say **SETPRINTER "LPT1"**.
- **SLEEP number** causes the PAL script to pause for the specified number of micro seconds. For example, the command **SLEEP 3000** tells the system to pause for 3 seconds because there are 1000 microseconds in a second.
- **SWITCH-CASE-ENDSWITCH** indicate the beginning and end of a decision area. Inside this area you will list a series of user options. If OTHERWISE is used and the user enters any data that is not one of the specified conditions, the commands after OTHERWISE are executed.
- **STRVAL(expression)** converts a numeric value to a string value. This command is often used to print the results of a calculation with descriptive text using only one print command. For example, if a program determines that there are 42 records in a database, that information could be printed easily with the command **?? "Number of records:" + STRVAL(42)**. In other words, the number 42 would be treated as text (called a string) rather than a numeric value.
- **TEXT-ENDTEXT** marks the beginning and the end of a block of text that will be displayed on the screen when the command executes.
- **WAIT-UNTIL** allows the user to examine or modify a field, record, table, or the workspace until the specified key is pressed. For example, the command structure **WAIT record UNTIL "DO_IT!"** will allow a user to change the data in a single record until the user presses F2 **(DO_IT!)**. The command **WAIT field UNTIL "DO_IT!"** would limit the user to a single field.
- **WHILE-ENDWHILE** marks the beginning and the end of a loop. The commands between these two statements are executed as long as the specified condition is met.

# ▶ E X E R C I S E

## EXERCISE 1

### CREATING A MENU PROGRAM FOR THE EMPLOYEE AND TIME FILES

Write a script file that presents a menu with choices to add records or edit records in the EMPLOYEE and TIME files. The script file should also include a choice to exit the program. Pattern your script file after the MENU script shown in the figure "The MENU.SC Script." When finished, make a printout of your script file.

# REVIEW

- To create and edit programs, open the SCRIPTS menu and select Editor.
- After entering or editing a program, press F2 **(DO_IT!)** to save your work and return to the Paradox main screen.
- Comment lines begin with a semicolon. These lines are ignored when the program is run, but can be used to document the program.
- To execute a PAL script, open the SCRIPTS menu and select Play.
- To make a printout of the program, load the script into the editor, open the FILE menu, and select Print.
- WHILE-ENDWHILE commands repeat all or part of a program until a specified condition is met.
- IF-ENDIF commands cause a program to branch based on the evaluation of a criteria. If the criteria is true, the program does one thing. If it is false, the program does another.
- SWITCH-CASE-ENDSWITCH commands provide a list of possible choices and branch the program depending on which choice is selected.
- TEXT and END TEXT statements identify the beginning and end of text blocks that are to be displayed on the screen.

# QUESTIONS

## FILL IN THE BLANK

1. To create or edit a command file named PROGRAM, you would open the _____ menu and choose _____.
2. To execute a command file named PROGRAM, you would open the _____ menu and choose _____.
3. To print the contents of a command file named PROGRAM, you would load the file into the editor, open the _____ menu, and select _____.
4. To have a series of commands repeat until a specified condition was met, you would use a _____ command.
5. To display a block of text on the screen, you would mark its beginning with _____ and its end with _____.
6. To have a program branch based on the evaluation of a criteria, you would use an _____ command.
7. To list a number of menu choices and have the program branch based on which choice is made, you could use a _____ command.

## MATCH THE COLUMNS

1. SCRIPTS-EDITOR command sequence
2. SCRIPTS-PLAY command sequence
3. F2 (DO_IT!)
4. END TEXT
5. WHILE-ENDWHILE
6. IF statements
7. SWITCH-CASE-ENDSWITCH
8. TEXT

___ Useful when entering lists of commands from which to choose

___ Executes a command file

___ Begins a block of text that is to appear on the screen

___ Saves a command file

___ Creates or edits a command file

___ Branches the program based on the evaluation of some criteria

___ Marks the beginning of a block of text that is to appear on the screen

___ Repeats a command or series of commands until a specified condition is met

## WRITE OUT THE ANSWERS

1. What command do you execute to write or edit a PAL script file?
2. What command do you execute to display the contents of a PAL script file?
3. What command do you use to execute a PAL script file?
4. What is a *variable*?

# CHAPTER 8

# Real-World Applications

Now that you are familiar with Paradox 4, you are ready to put it to work. The applications in this chapter include a job-search kit, a research paper, and a business plan. These projects test and build on the skills that you have already acquired.

> **When completing the applications, keep the following points in mind.**
> - The applications are based on the procedures already discussed in the text, but they present new problems for you to solve on your own. Don't give up! It may take some thought and effort to work through them.
> - The Concepts section in each application gives you all of the subject area information you will need to complete the application.
> - The Steps section in each application gives you the sequence of steps that you should follow. If you cannot remember how to perform a procedure, refer to the topic that covers that material.

---

**APPLICATION 1**

## The Job-Search Kit—Company Contacts

To find a job in today's employment market, you must be organized and relentless in the pursuit of possible employers. Accurate record keeping and effective followup may be the key to your success. Every interview should be followed by a well-written letter that emphasizes your strong points. In this application, you create a database that can organize your search and make your follow-up easier and more effective.

---

### CONCEPTS

When you are looking for employment, you need to tip the balance in your favor at every opportunity. First, do a little research about the company that you want to contact. You need to know something about who they are and what they do so that you can write an effective cover letter and "fine tune" your resume. Most importantly, try to send your resume to a specific individual, by name. Sending a letter to a company or to the personnel department is a sure sign that you have not done your research.

Unfortunately, most published corporate listings are out of date. Call the company and find out the name of the person that should receive your application. For example, if you are applying for a sales position, call the sales department and ask the person that answers the phone for the name, title, and address of the person who makes the hiring decisions. You can then send your resume to that person, by name, and follow up with a phone call to make sure that the letter arrived. Be sure that you get the correct spelling of the name and the correct address. Finally, save that information in your database file for future reference and followup.

**S T E P S**

1. Look at the records shown in the figure "The JOBSRCH Records" and use them to plan a database with the fields listed in the table "The JOBSRCH Database." Before you enter any actual data, indicate each field's name, its type, and its length.

### THE JOBSRCH DATABASE

| Description | Field's name | Type and Width |
|---|---|---|
| Company name | _____ | _____ |
| Company street | _____ | _____ |
| Company city | _____ | _____ |
| Company state | _____ | _____ |
| Company zip code | _____ | _____ |
| Contact's salutation (Mr., Mrs., or Ms.) | _____ | _____ |
| Contact's first name | _____ | _____ |
| Contact's last name | _____ | _____ |
| Date of first interview | _____ | _____ |
| Date of second interview | _____ | _____ |
| Date of third interview | _____ | _____ |
| Job offered (Y/N) | _____ | _____ |
| Starting salary offered | _____ | _____ |
| Comments | _____ | _____ |

2. Create a database named JOBSRCH and use the information from Step 1 to define its structure.
3. List the file's structure to the printer.
4. Enter the records shown in the figure "The JOBSRCH Records."
5. Add the records in the JOBHOLD file to your database. The JOBHOLD file can be found on your *Resource Disk.*
6. List the file's records to the printer. Proofread the printout and then edit the records if necessary.
7. List on the printer only the companies that offered a job.
8. Calculate the average salary offered. Remember, only include the records in which the salary was greater than zero.

**JOBSRCH Records**

Enter these records into the JOBSRCH database after it is defined.

| | Company 1 | Company 2 | Company 3 |
|---|---|---|---|
| **Firm** | Marble Harbor Press | ComputerPlace | The Driftwood |
| **Street** | 100 Atlantic Avenue | 16010 Adams Street | 4 Front Street |
| **City** | Marblehead | Fresno | Boca Raton |
| **State** | MA | CA | FL |
| **ZIP code** | 01945 | 93710 | 33433 |
| **Salutation** | Mr. | Ms. | Mr. |
| **First name** | William | Matilda | Richard |
| **Last name** | Kinsman | Smith | Ashley |
| **Resume sent** | 1/6/94 | 1/6/94 | 1/6/94 |
| **Interview 1** | 3/10/94 | 3/15/94 | 5/11/94 |
| **Interview 2** | 4/20/94 | | 5/13/94 |
| **Interview 3** | | | 5/18/94 |
| **Offer?** | Yes | No | Yes |
| **Salary** | $19,000 | | $20,000 |
| **Comments** | I like the office environment | | I'll take it! |

9. List the contact's name and address to the printer for every company that offered a job.

10. Prepare mailing labels that print out just people that interviewed you. The labels should include the person's name (using their salutation) and the name and address of their firm. Print the labels on the printer.

11. Sort the database by zip code and print the labels again.

12. Copy the file's structure to a file called MYJOBS so that you can use it in your own job search.

---

## The Research Paper—Works Cited

Many types of documents, including research papers, must have a bibliography or list of works cited that shows publication information about each of the documents that were used as sources. Traditionally, you would write each publication on a filing card and then manually alphabetize them. In this application, you will create a database that can be used to update your sources easily and arrange them in order by indexing or sorting.

---

**CONCEPTS**

The term *documentation style* refers to the various systems used to display the sources used in a research paper. Documentation styles vary among the disciplines. Some styles use footnotes, others use endnotes, and some even put the reference information in parentheses within the text.

Before you start consulting your sources, you need to know what documentation style will be needed for your paper. (If your assignment does not specify a documentation style, check with your instructor.) Be aware of what information your documentation style requires. Then, as you take notes, keep a record of that information so that you can document your sources fully and accurately.

The **Modern Language Association (MLA)** has developed the documentation styles used in most of the humanities. Before 1984, the "MLA style" required footnotes or endnotes and a list of sources called the *Bibliography*. The current MLA style, introduced in 1984, calls for parenthetical references instead of footnotes or endnotes. It also changed the name of the list of sources to *Works Cited*. This list includes only the sources from which you used paraphrases or quotes. It does not include sources that you consulted but did not actually refer to in the paper. This list follows any endnotes and begins on a new page, numbered sequentially with the rest of the paper. Entries are alphabetized and start at the left margin. The second, and subsequent, lines of each entry indent five spaces (1/2 inch). Double spacing is used within and between the entries.

The **American Psychological Association (APA)** has developed another documentation style commonly used for research papers, especially in the social sciences. Like the MLA style, the APA style uses parenthetical references and a list of sources. In this application, the sources will be listed in MLA style but, if necessary, you can easily adapt the information to the APA style.

---

## ► S T E P S

Curtin, Dennis. <u>Microcomputers: Software and Applications</u>. Englewood Cliffs: Prentice, 1989.

Burks, Alice R., and Arthur W. Burks. <u>The First Electronic Computer: The Atanasoff Story</u>. Ann Arbor: U of Michigan P, 1988.

Hollerbach, Lew. <u>A 60-minute Guide to Microcomputers</u>. 1st American ed. Englewood Cliffs: Prentice, 1982.

Forester, Tom, ed. <u>The Information Technology Revolution</u>. Cambridge: MIT P, 1985.

Dubbey, John Michael. <u>The Mathematical Work of Charles Babbage</u>. Cambridge UP, 1978.

Bashe, Charles J., et al. <u>IBM's Early Computers</u>. Cambridge: MIT P, 1986.

Gorstine, G.W. <u>16 Bit Modern Microcomputers: The Intel I8086 Family</u>. Englewood Cliffs: Prentice, 1985.

**The TERMPAPR Records**
Enter these records into the TERMPAPR database after it is defined.

1. Look at the sources shown in the figure "The TERMPAPR Records" and use them to plan a database with the fields listed in the table "The TERMPAPR Database." Decide on a name for each field, what type it needs to be, and its length.

### THE TERMPAPR DATABASE

| Description | Field's name | Type and Width |
|---|---|---|
| Author's name | _____ | _____ |
| Title of book | _____ | _____ |
| City in which book was published | _____ | _____ |
| Name of publisher | _____ | _____ |
| Copyright date | _____ | _____ |
| Cited in paper (Y/N) | _____ | _____ |
| Comments | _____ | _____ |

2. Create a database named TERMPAPR and use the information from Step 1 to define its structure.
3. List the file's structure to the printer.
4. Enter the records shown in the figure "The TERMPAPR Records." Show all records as "cited" except for records two and five.
5. List the file's records to the printer. Proofread the printout and then edit the records if necessary.
6. List to the printer all books published in Englewood Cliffs.

7. List to the printer all books published in Cambridge.
8. Prepare a report format named TERMPAPR that prints out only the author and the title of each work. Print your report on the printer.
9. Key the file according to the author's last name. Print the file again, but this time only display the works that were actually cited.
10. Copy the file's structure to a new file named MYPAPER so that it can be used for your own term papers or other library research.

## APPLICATION 3

# The Business Plan—Inventory Records

A business must control its inventory or you will not be able to provide maximum service at the lowest possible cost. Your aim is to achieve a rapid turnover of your inventory. The less money and space that is tied up in raw materials, work in progress, and finished goods, the better. In other words, if you recover your investment quickly, you can reinvest your capitol for other business purposes.

The average firm has 15 to 25% of its capital invested in inventory. In addition, the cost of a large inventory can be as high as 35% of the average inventory value. The benefits of a reduced inventory are clear.

A manufacturer that carries $300,000 in inventory will probably pay more than $60,000 a year in carrying costs. Reducing inventory not only frees capital invested in inventory, but also reduces carrying costs. A good rule of thumb for inventory control is to carry only the inventory needed to provide good service and to supply materials to production so that interruptions do not occur.

## ▶ STEPS

1. Look at the sources shown in the figure "The INVENTRY Records" and use them to plan a database with the fields listed in the table "The INVENTRY Database." Decide on a name for each field, what type it needs to be and its length.

### THE INVENTRY DATABASE

| Description | Field's name | Type and Width |
|---|---|---|
| Part's stock number | | |
| Part's name | | |
| Part's description | | |
| Part's cost | | |
| Order date | | |
| Instock date | | |
| Quantity in order | | |
| Quantity received | | |
| Unit cost | | |

2. Create a database named INVENTRY and use the information from Step 1 to define its structure.
3. List the file's structure to the printer.
4. Enter the records shown in the figure "The INVENTRY Records."

|  | Part 1 | Part 2 | Part 3 |
|---|---|---|---|
| Manufacturer | IBM | Compaq | HP |
| Description | Hard disk drive | Tower computer | ScanJet |
| Stock number | 10010 | MD50 | L300 |
| Unit cost | 325 | 1250 | 1200 |
| Order date | 9/10/94 | 9/11/94 | 9/11/94 |
| Instock date | 9/20/94 | 9/25/94 | 9/20/94 |
| Qty. ordered | 75 | 5 | 10 |
| Qty. received | 73 | 5 | 10 |
| Selling price | 650 | 2500 | 1800 |

5. Add the records in the INVHOLD file to your database. The INVHOLD file can be found on your *Resource Disk.*
6. List the file's records to the printer. Proofread the printout and then edit the records if necessary.
7. List to the printer any record where the quantity received is less than the quantity ordered.
8. List to the printer any record where the number of days between ordering and receiving is greater than seven days.
9. Calculate the total inventory cost for each item by multiplying the quantity received by the unit cost. Print the results on the printer.
10. Prepare a stock report named INVENTRY that prints out only the stock number, the unit cost, the quantity received, and the selling price.
11. Key the file by stock number and print the report again.

# N O T E S

# NOTES

# DOS—An Overview

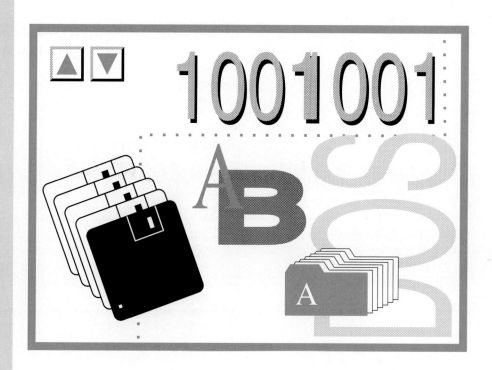

# DOS—An Overview

To use a computer, you must first load the operating system. This is called booting the system. The term *booting* comes from the expression "pulling oneself up by one's bootstraps." Once the operating system is loaded, you can load your application programs or use the operating system's commands to manage your files and disks.

If your computer is off, you load the operating system by turning it on. When you do so, the computer automatically looks to the startup drive for the operating system files that it needs to start up.

- On a floppy disk system, the startup drive is drive A, so you have to insert a disk that contains the operating system files into that drive.
- On a hard disk system, the startup drive is drive C, but the computer still looks to drive A first. Therefore, before you turn on a hard disk system, be sure to open the door to drive A or eject any disk that is in it so that the program does not try to load the operating system from that drive (see the box "Things That Can Go Wrong").

If the files it needs to start are on the disk in the startup drive, that disk is called a *system disk*. If the files are not on the disk in the startup drive, an error message is displayed, and the system will not boot.

Turning a computer on to boot it is called a cold boot. However, you can also reboot a computer if it is already on—called warm booting. To warm-boot the system, you hold down [Ctrl] and [Alt] and then press [Del]. (This command is usually written out as **Ctrl**-**Alt**-**Del**.). Warm booting clears all data from the computer's memory and has almost the same effect as turning the computer off and then back on again. You normally use this procedure only when you encounter a problem with your system. Whenever possible, you should exit any application program you are using before warm booting your system, or you may lose data.

---

**THINGS THAT CAN GO WRONG**

It is not at all likely that anything you type on a computer will really harm the system, but it is easy to make mistakes that affect your own work. That's why you should always keep backup copies of important files and take care to follow the directions in this text as you enter commands that are new to you. Here are some problems to look out for when working with DOS:

- When you boot an IBM computer system, you may see the error message *Non-System disk or disk error* (or a similar message on compatible computers). This appears when you turn on the computer with a disk in drive A that does not contain the operating system files that the computer needs. If you get this message, insert the DOS disk into drive A or open the drive's door if it is a hard disk system, and press [Enter ←⏎].

■ The message *Bad command or filename* appears when you type a command incorrectly or when DOS cannot find the file you have tried to run. If you get this prompt, retype the command, or find a disk with the DOS utility program that you want to use.

■ If you make a typo and notice it before you press [Enter ←⏎], press [← Bksp] to delete it, and then retype it.

■ If you or the computer addresses a drive (for example, type **A:** and press [Enter ←⏎]) and the drive doesn't contain a disk, a message tells you the computer is not ready reading the drive and then offers you options to *abort, retry, fail,* or *ignore* (although the choices vary depending on the version of DOS you are using).

- *Abort* cancels the command and returns you to the command prompt (or Shell).

- *Retry* retries the command, perhaps after you have closed a drive door or inserted a disk.

- *Fail* cancels the current portion of the command and then continues.

- *Ignore* ignores the problem and continues processing the command.

■ To cancel a command in progress, press [Ctrl]-[C] or [Ctrl]-[Break].

## TUTORIAL

In this tutorial, you take a quick guided tour of some of the most commonly used DOS procedures. You load DOS, check which version you are using, format a disk so that you can store your own work on it, explore directories, and copy files.

To load DOS on some systems, such as those connected to networks or with special startup menus, you follow procedures specific to your system. In these cases, ask your instructor how to display the DOS command prompt, and then start this tutorial at the section headed "Changing the Command Prompt."

---

**LOADING DOS ON YOUR OWN SYSTEM**

Many computers are now networked or have other special startup procedures. If your system is one of these, list the steps here that you use to access the DOS command prompt so that you have them for future reference.

1. _____

2. _____

3. _____

4. _____

5. _____

---

## GETTING STARTED

1. If your computer is on, turn it off. The location of the On/Off switch varies, but it may be located on the right side of the computer toward the rear.
2. Before proceeding:
   - If you are working on a hard disk system, open the door to drive A or eject the disk in that drive. Drive A is the name of the floppy drive if there is only one. If there are two (or more) drives, drive A is usually the one on the top or on the left.
   - If you are working on a floppy disk system, insert the DOS disk into drive A. If there are two (or more) drives, drive A is usually the one on the top or on the left. (On some systems, there may be more than one DOS disk. If you are working on such a system, the disk you use to boot the computer might be named the DOS startup, boot, or system disk. If you are unsure of which disk to use, ask.)

## LOADING THE OPERATING SYSTEM

3. Turn on the computer. In a few moments, the computer may beep, and then drive A spins, and its light comes on while the operating system is loaded. If there is no disk in drive A, the computer looks to drive C for the program if the system contains a hard disk drive.
   - If a list of files is displayed, and the screen has the title *MS-DOS Shell*, *IBM DOS Shell*, or *Start Programs*, press [F3] to display the command prompt.
   - If nothing appears on your screen, your display screen may not be on. On some systems, the display screen has a separate On/Off switch.
   - If your computer does not have a clock that is set automatically, in a moment the prompt reads *Enter new date:*. If this prompt appears, refer to the box "Entering or Changing the Date and Time."

   The command prompt appears and should read *C:\>*, *C>*, *C:\DOS>*, *A:\>*, *A>*, or something similar. This prompt indicates that DOS has been loaded.

---

### ENTERING OR CHANGING THE DATE AND TIME

When you first turn on some computers, you are prompted to enter the date and time. Entering the correct date and time is important because the computer's clock date-and-time-marks files that you save. The clock is also used by some programs to enter dates and times into files and to display them on the screen.

If you are prompted to enter the date, type it in the format MM-DD-YY, where MM (month) is a number from 1 to 12, DD (day) is a number from 1 to 31, and YY (year) is a number from 80 to 99 or from 1980 to 1999. For example, to enter the date January 10, 1993, type 1-10-93 and press [Enter←].

To enter the time when prompted to do so, use the format HH:MM, where HH (hours) is a number between 0 and 23, and MM (minutes) is a number between 0 and 59. For example, to set the clock to 1:30

---

p.m., type **13:30** and press ⌨Enter↵. If you are using DOS 4 or later, you could also enter it as 1:30p (for p.m.).

## CHANGING THE COMMAND PROMPT

4. If your command prompt does not read *C:\>*, *C:\DOS>*, or *A:\>*, type **PROMPT $P$G** and press ⌨Enter↵ so that it does (although the *DOS* part may be different).

## CHECKING THE VERSION NUMBER

5. Type **VER** and press ⌨Enter↵ to display the version number of the operating system you are using. Write it down so that you don't forget it. The commands you use vary somewhat depending on which version of DOS your system is running.

## FORMATTING A DATA DISK

6. Locate a blank disk that **DOES NOT** contain any valuable files. The command you are about to use effectively erases all data from the disk.

7. Insert your disks as follows:
   - On a hard disk system, insert the blank disk into drive A.
   - On a floppy disk system with two disk drives, insert the DOS disk into drive A and the blank disk into drive B.

8. Set your drives as follows:
   - On a hard disk system, type **C:** and press ⌨Enter↵ to change the default drive to drive C. The command prompt should read *C:\>* or *C:\DOS>*.
   - On a floppy disk system, type **A:** and press ⌨Enter↵ to change the default drive to drive A. The command prompt should read *A:\>*.

9. Enter the FORMAT command as follows:
   - On a hard disk system, type **FORMAT A:** and press ⌨Enter↵.
   - On a floppy disk system, type **FORMAT B:** and press ⌨Enter↵.
   In a moment, a prompt asks you to insert a disk into the drive you entered in the FORMAT command and press or strike ⌨Enter↵ when ready. You already inserted the disks in a previous step. (If you get the message *Bad command or filename*, or something similar, ask your instructor on what disk or in which directory the FORMAT.COM file can be found, and insert that disk or ask how you change to that directory.)

10. Press ⌨Enter↵, and the drive spins as it formats the disk. (On DOS 4 and later versions, a message on the screen keeps you posted on the progress.) When the message reads *Format complete*, the drive stops.

11. If you are using DOS 4 or a later version, you are prompted to enter a volume label. Type your last name (abbreviate to 11 characters if necessary), and press ⌨Enter↵ to continue.)

12. When the prompt reads *Format another (Y/N)?*, press N̄ and then press ⌨Enter↵.

## NOTE: ENTERING COMMANDS

- In all the instructions in this text, the characters you type are shown in upper-case letters, but whether you use uppercase or lowercase letters usually does not matter. For example, you can type **PROMPT $P$G** or **prompt $p$g**.
- If you make a typo when entering any commands, press ⌨←Bksp to delete the incorrect characters, and then type them in correctly before pressing ⌨Enter↵.

## NOTE: DEFAULT DRIVES

Most computers have more than one disk drive. For this reason, disks are assigned names: A, B, C, and so on. Just as you can be in only one place at a time, so it is for your computer. It is always on one and only one of the drives. The drive it is on is called the *default drive*. To have a command affect a disk in any other drive, you must indicate the letter of that drive in the command. This is called *addressing* the drive.

## NOTE: DIRECTORIES

Disks can store a lot of files. To keep them organized, experienced users divide the disk into directories that are like file folders in which related files can be stored. Knowing which directory a file is in is important since you may not be able to run a program or copy a file unless you do. Think of directories as an address. Just as you may live in San Francisco in the state of California, a file may be stored in a directory named DOS on a drive named C.

### EXPLORING YOUR STUDENT RESOURCE DISK

13. Insert the *Student Resource Disk* into drive A. (The *Student Resource Disk* is a special disk that contains all the files you need to complete many of the tutorials and exercises in this text.)

14. Type **A:** and press [Enter←] to change the default drive to A, and the command prompt reads *A:\>*.

15. Type **DIR** and press [Enter←] to list the directories on the disk. Directories are like file folders in which you can store related files. They are used to organize your work and programs on the disk. You can tell that DOS and WP51 are directories, for example, because they are followed by the notation *<DIR>*.

16. Type **CD \DOS** and press [Enter←] to move to the DOS directory.

17. Type **DIR** and press [Enter←] to display a list of the files in the DOS directory along with information about each file. The list is too long to be displayed on the screen, so the topmost files scroll off the top. However, notice how each file has a name such as WHATSUP, an extension such as DOC, a size (in bytes), a date, and a time.

18. Type **DIR/W** and press [Enter←] to display the filenames in five columns without additional information so that more names can be displayed at one time.

19. Type **CD \WP51** and press [Enter←] to move to the WP51 directory.

20. Type **DIR** and press [Enter←] to display a list of the files in that directory.

21. Type **CD \DOS** and press [Enter←] to return to the DOS directory.

22. Type **DIR *.DOC** and press [Enter←] to display one file, named WHATSUP.DOC. The command told DOS to list any file with a period followed by the three letters DOC.

### COPYING FILES

23. Type **COPY *.* A:\** and press [Enter←] to copy all the files from the DOS directory to A:\, the topmost directory on the disk—called the *root directory*. Files are listed on the screen as they are copied, and when all have been copied, the command prompt reappears. The *.* (called star-dot-star) part of the command uses wildcards to tell DOS "all files."

24. Type **DIR** and press [Enter←] to see that all the files are still in the DOS directory.

25. Type **CD \** and press [Enter←] to move back up to the root directory. The command prompt should change to A:\ to indicate that you are there.

26. Type **DIR** and press [Enter←] to see that copies of all the files that were in the DOS directory are now in the root directory.

### FINISHING UP

27. Either continue to the next activity or quit for the day. When you are done for the day, you should always exit the program you are using to return to the operating system, and then:
    - Open the floppy disk drive doors or eject the disks in the drives

so that the disk drives' read/write heads don't leave indentations in the disks' surfaces.

■ Remove your disks from the disk drives to prevent their loss, increase security, and ensure that no one mistakenly erases them.

■ Turn off the computer or use the display monitor's controls to dim the screen so that an image will not be "burned" into its phosphor surface.

*Quick Reference*

> FORMATTING

When you open a box of new floppy disks, they will usually not work properly on your computer because they have been designed to work with a variety of computer systems. To customize them so that they will work with the equipment you are using, you format the disks. Formatting checks the disk surface for unusable spots, divides the disk into tracks and sectors, and creates a directory.

Formatting a disk effectively erases any data that may already have been saved on it. You therefore have to be careful with this command. You should never format a previously used disk unless you are sure you will not need any of the files on it. Moreover, you should never format a hard disk drive unless you are willing to lose every file on the disk. However, since no one is perfect and mistakes do happen, DOS 5 added an unformat command that helps you recover files should you format a disk by mistake.

When you format a disk, the operating system divides it into tracks and sectors, an invisible magnetic pattern something like a dart board. On a formatted disk, tracks run in circles around the disk. Because tracks can store a great deal of data, the computer needs to divide them into sectors, which makes it easier to find a location on the disk. These sectors are like pie-shaped wedges that divide each track into the same number of sectors.

To store more data, the tracks on the disk are placed closer together. The spacing of these tracks is measured as tracks per inch (TPI). The number of TPI determines the density of the disk and the amount of data that can be stored on it. A high-density disk has more tracks per inch than a low-density disk and can therefore store more data. The maximum density that can be used to store data on a disk is indicated on the disk label and box. For example, on 5¼-inch disks:

- Double-density disks can store data on 48 TPI or up to 360KB.
- High-density disks (also called high-capacity or quad-density disks) can store data on 96 TPI or up to 1.2MB.

The smaller 3½-inch floppy disks can store 720KB or 1.44MB. These disks can store more data than the larger 5¼-inch disks because they can store data on 135 TPI. You can tell the two types of disks apart as follows:

- A 720KB disk is labeled 1.0MB or 2HC and has a single square cutout.
- A 1.44MB disk is labeled 2.0MB or HD and has two square cutouts.

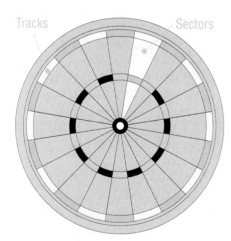

Tracks    Sectors

**A Formatted Disk**
One way to visualize a formatted disk is as a dart board. Tracks run in circles around the disk. The number of tracks per inch determines the density of the disk. A high-density disk has more tracks per inch than a low-density disk and can therefore store more data. Since the tracks can store a great deal of data, the computer divides them into sectors, which makes it easier to find a location on the disk. These sectors are like pie-shaped wedges that radiate from the center of the disk.

## FORMATTING AND READING 5¼-INCH DISKS

| Procedure | 360KB Drive | 1.2MB Drive |
|---|---|---|
| Format a 360KB disk | Yes | Yes* |
| Format a 1.2MB disk | No | Yes |
| Read a 360KB disk | Yes | Yes |
| Read a 1.2MB disk | No | Yes |

\* With switches

## FORMATTING AND READING 3½-INCH DISKS

| Procedure | 720KB Drive | 1.44MB Drive |
|---|---|---|
| Format a 720KB disk | Yes | Yes* |
| Format a 1.44MB disk | No | Yes |
| Read a 720KB disk | Yes | Yes |
| Read a 1.44MB disk | No | Yes |

\* With switches

### NOTE: SWITCHES

Many DOS commands have options you can specify to control or vary the results. To tell DOS to use these options, you add switches to the commands. Most switches are specified by typing a slash followed by a letter or number. For example, to format a 360KB disk in a 1.2MB disk drive, you would use the command FORMAT/4 instead of simply FORMAT.

Because of these variations in the way computers assign tracks and sectors, the disks you use must be appropriate for your system. Some of the possible combinations are shown in the tables "Formatting and Reading 5¼-Inch Disks" and "Formatting and Reading 3½-Inch Disks."

To format a data disk, you use the FORMAT command. The FORMAT.COM file must be on one of the drives since this is an external command.

DOS always formats a disk to match the drive it is being formatted in unless you specify otherwise. To change the way a disk is formatted, you add switches to the FORMAT command to control the formatting process. For example, you may want to format a 360KB disk in a 1.2MB drive or a 720KB 3½-inch disk in a 1.44MB drive. To format a 360KB disk in a 1.2MB 5¼-inch drive, use the command FORMAT <drive:> / 4. To format a 720KB disk in a 1.44MB 3½-inch drive, use the command FORMAT <drive:> /F:720.

→ **K E Y / S t r o k e s**

### Formatting Floppy Disks

1. Insert your disks as follows:
   - On a hard disk system, insert the disk to be formatted into drive A.
   - On a floppy disk system, insert the disk with the file FORMAT.COM into drive A and the disk to be formatted into drive B.
2. Set your drives as follows:
   - On a hard disk system, make drive C the default drive.
   - On a floppy disk system, make drive A the default drive.
3. Enter the command as follows:
   - On a hard disk system, type **FORMAT A:** and press Enter←┘.
   - On a floppy disk system, type **FORMAT B:** and press Enter←┘.

   In a moment, a prompt asks you to insert a disk into the drive you entered in the FORMAT command and press or strike Enter←┘ when ready. You inserted the disks in Step 1.
4. Press Enter←┘ to continue and the drive spins as it formats the disk. On DOS 4 and later versions, a message is displayed on the screen to keep you posted on the progress. (DOS 5 also saves UNFORMAT information.) When the message reads *Format complete*, the drive stops.

   If you are using DOS 4 or later, a prompt reads *Volume label (11 characters, ENTER for none)?*. Either type a volume name to identify the disk and press Enter←┘ or press Enter←┘ without entering a volume name.

   The prompt reads *Format another (Y/N)?*.
5. Either: Press N and then Enter←┘ to quit formatting and return to the command prompt.

   Or: Insert a new disk into the same drive as you did in Step 1, press Y and then Enter←┘ to display the prompt asking you to insert a new disk. Press the designated key to continue.

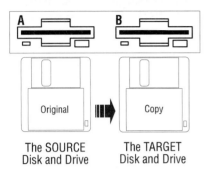

The SOURCE
Disk and Drive

The TARGET
Disk and Drive

**Source and Target Drives**

The source drive is the one containing the files you want to copy. The target drive is the one you want them copied to.

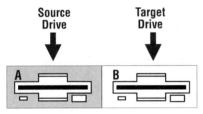

Source
Drive

Target
Drive

COPY FILENAME.EXT B:

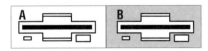

COPY A:FILENAME.EXT

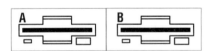

COPY A:FILENAME.EXT B:

**Specifying Drives in Commands**

Three possible copying situations are illustrated here. In the first, the source drive is the default (shown tinted), so you need to specify only the target drive in a command. In the second, the target drive is the default, so you need to specify only the source drive in a command. In the third, neither drive is the default, so you must specify both the source and target drives in a command.

To copy one or more files from one disk to another, you use the COPY command. This command is often used to make backup copies of important files.

When you use this command, you usually must specify three things:

1. The drive containing the disk the files are to be copied from—the source drive unless it is the default drive.
2. The name of the files to be copied.
3. The drive containing the disk the files are to be copied to—the target drive unless it is the default drive.

Keep in mind that the source is the drive containing the disk that you want the action performed on. The target is the drive containing the disk that you want to be affected by the source. For example, to copy a file from drive A to drive B, you use the command COPY A:FILENAME.EXT B:. The A: specifies the source drive that contains the file to be copied, and the B: specifies the target drive that you want the file copied to.

If your system has only one floppy disk drive, specify the source drive as drive A and the target drive as drive B. The operating system will then prompt you to swap disks whenever it needs access to the source or target disk and it is not in the drive.

The COPY command is an internal command that you can use to copy single files or groups of files. When using it, you must specify the source and target drives only if they are not the default drives. For example:

- If the default drive is set to A, and you want to copy a file named LETTER on drive A to drive B, you would type **COPY LETTER B:**. This command reads "copy the file named LETTER in the default drive to drive B." You do not need to specify drive A because that is the default drive.
- If the default drive is set to B, and you want to copy a file named LETTER on drive A to drive B, you would type **COPY A:LETTER**. The command reads "copy the file named LETTER in drive A to the default drive." You do not need to specify drive B because that is the default drive.

### ➜ K E Y / S t r o k e s

**Copying Files**

1. Insert your disks as follows:
   - On a hard disk system, insert the source disk into drive A. You will be prompted to swap disks periodically.
   - On a floppy disk system, insert the source disk into drive A and the target disk into drive B.
2. Either: Type **COPY A:*.* B:** and press Enter↵ to copy all files.
   Or: Type **COPY A:**<*filename.ext*> **B:** and press Enter↵ to copy a single file.

- Regardless of which drive is the default, you can specify both the source and target drives as a precaution. For example, to copy the file named LETTER from drive A to drive B regardless of which drive is the default drive, type **COPY A:LETTER B:**. This command reads "copy the file named LETTER in drive A to drive B."

If you copy a file to a disk or directory that already has a file by the same name, the copied file overwrites and replaces the original file.

## DELETING FILES

To delete one or more files, you use the ERASE or DEL command. These two internal commands are interchangeable—they work exactly alike. For example, to delete a file on drive B named FILENAME.EXT, you type either **ERASE B:FILENAME.EXT** or **DEL B:FILENAME.EXT** and press Enter⏎.

You can use wildcards with the ERASE and DEL commands, but it is dangerous to do so. Even a slight miscalculation can cause the wrong files to be deleted. However, there are precautions you can take:

- One way to use wildcards safely is to preview what files will be affected by specifying the planned wildcards in the DIR command. If only the files you want to delete are listed, the same wildcards are safe to use with the ERASE or DEL command. For example, if you want to delete all files with the extension .BAK, type **DIR \*.BAK**. If the displayed list of files can all be deleted, type **DEL \*.BAK** (or type **DEL** and press F3).
- To be prompted for each file when using DOS 4 or later, use the /P switch. For example, to delete all files with the extension .BAK, type **DEL \*.BAK/P**. Before each file is deleted, a prompt reads *Delete (Y/N)?*. Press Y to delete the file, or press N to leave the file on the disk.
- If you use the \*.\* wildcards, a prompt reads *Are you sure (Y/N)?*. Press Y to continue and delete all the files, or press N to cancel the command.

### → KEY/Strokes

**Deleting Files from the Disk**

1. Select the name of the file you want to delete, and make the drive that it's on the default drive.
2. Type **ERASE** <*filename*> or **DEL** <*filename*> and press Enter⏎.

## USING DIRECTORIES

Dividing a disk into directories helps you organize your files better. Imagine using a file drawer to store all of your memos, letters, and reports. Before long, the drawer would become so crowded and disorganized that you could not find anything. But with a little organization and planning, the documents could be organized into folders, making it easier to locate the one you needed.

A disk is like an empty drawer in a new filing cabinet: It provides a lot of storage space but no organization. To make it easier to find items in the drawer, you can divide it into categories with hanging folders. You can file documents directly into the hanging folders, or you can divide them into finer categories with manila folders. A directory is like a hanging folder, and a subdirectory is like a manila folder within a hanging folder. A file in a directory or subdirectory is like a letter, report, or other document within either a hanging folder or a manila folder.

Directories on a disk drive are organized in a hierarchy. The main directory, the one not below any other directory, is the root directory. Below it, directories can be created on one or more levels. These directories can hold files or subdirectories. The terms *directory* and *subdirectory* are used somewhat loosely. Strictly speaking, there is only one directory—the root directory—and all others are subdirectories. In most discussions, however, any directory above another is called a directory, and those below it are called its subdirectories.

Any disk may be divided into directories and subdirectories. You will often find floppy disks with directories, and almost every hard disk has them. To work with these disks, you have to know how to move between directories and see how they are organized.

To change directories on the current drive, you use the CHDIR or CD command. To change the default directory, type **CD**\<*drive:\directory*> and press Enter←. If you are changing more than one level, list the directories in order, separated by a backslash. There are several versions of these commands. For example, in the figure "Moving Through Directories," the following commands would work:

- To make the subdirectory OLD the default directory, you would type **CD\LETTERS\OLD** and press Enter←.
- To move up one directory, for example, from OLD to LETTERS, you would type **CD..** and press Enter←.
- To move down to a subdirectory within the current directory, for example, from LETTERS to NEW, you would type **CD NEW**.
- To return to the root directory from any other directory, you would type **CD\** and press Enter←.

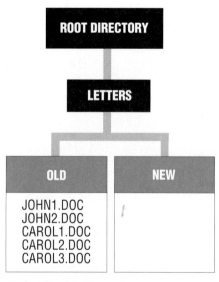

**Moving Through Directories**
This figure shows the root directory, a LETTERS directory, and two subdirectories, OLD and NEW.

→ **K E Y / S t r o k e s**

**Changing Directories**

- To move to a directory, type **CD**\<*directory*> and press Enter←.
- To return to the root directory, type **CD\** and press Enter←.
- To move up one level, type **CD..** and press Enter←.
- To move down one level, type **CD** <*directory*> and press Enter←.
- To display the current directory, type **CD** and press Enter←.
- To display the default directory on drive C, type **CD C:** and press Enter←.

To display the default directory on the current drive, type **CD** and press ⌷Enter↵⌷. To display the current default directory on another drive, type **CD** followed by the drive identifier, and press ⌷Enter↵⌷. For example, to display the current directory on drive C, type **CD C:** and press ⌷Enter↵⌷.

### Changing the Command Prompt

The default command prompt (which you get if you type **PROMPT** and press ⌷Enter↵⌷) is the letter of the current default drive followed by a greater-than sign, but you type **PROMPT $P$G** and press ⌷Enter↵⌷ to display the current drive and directory.

## ➤ S P E C I F Y I N G    P A T H S

When a disk is divided into directories, you not only must specify a drive, you also must specify a directory or directories in many commands. Specifying the drive and directories is called specifying a path.

Paths are simply a listing of the directories and subdirectories that specify exactly where a file can be found or where it is to be copied to. It is like telling someone that "the letter to ACME Hardware is in the manila folder labeled ACME in the hanging folder labeled Hardware in the third file cabinet from the right." These precise instructions make it easy to locate the file.

To specify a path, you must indicate the drive, then the name of all subdirectories leading to the file, and then the filename. All elements must be separated from one another by backslashes (\), for example, C:\LETTER\NEW\FILE1.DOC.

When specifying paths, you have to consider both the source and target directories:

- If the source directory is the default, you have to specify only the source filename and the path to the target.
- If the target directory is the default, you have to specify only the path to the source and the source filename.
- If neither the target nor the source directory is the default, you have to specify the path for both.

For example, let's assume your disk has the directories and files shown in the figure "Specifying Paths."

- To copy files, you have to specify a path only when the source or target directory is not the default.
  - When OLD is the default, the path you specify to copy FILE1 to the NEW directory is only for the target. For example, type **COPY FILE1 C:\NEW**.
  - When NEW is the default, the path you specify to copy FILE1 to the NEW directory is only for the source. For example, type **COPY C:\OLD\FILE1**.
  - When the root directory is the default, the paths you specify to copy FILE1 to the NEW directory are for both the source and the target. For example, type **COPY C:\OLD\FILE1 C:\NEW**.

- To display a list of the filenames in a directory, the same principles work.

Drive Identifier

**A: \ Directory \ Subdirectory**

Backslash | Backslash
Directory Name | Subdirectory Name

**Specifying Paths**
When specifying a path, you use a drive identifier and then list a directory and any subdirectories. Each item is separated from the next by a backslash.

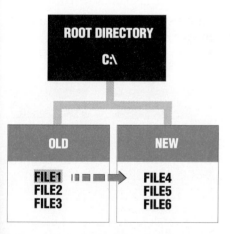

COPY C:\OLD\FILE1 C:\NEW

**Paths**
When copying files, displaying directories, or deleting files from the command prompt, you have to specify a path when the source or target directory is not the default.

- When the root directory is the default, you can display its directory by just typing **DIR** and pressing [Enter←].
- To display the files in the OLD directory, you type **DIR C:\OLD** and press [Enter←].
- To display the files in the NEW directory, you type **DIR C:\NEW** and press [Enter←].

■ To delete a file, the same principles also work. For example, when OLD is the default directory:

- To delete FILE1, you type **DEL FILE1** and press [Enter←].
- To delete FILE4 in the NEW subdirectory, you type **DEL C:\NEW\FILE4** and press [Enter←].

## MANAGING DIRECTORIES

To organize your work on a hard disk drive, you create directories. When the directories are no longer needed, you remove them (after deleting all the files they contain).

### Making Directories

To make a directory, you use the internal command MKDIR <*directory name*> (or MD <*directory name*>). Directory names follow the same conventions that you use for filenames. However, you should not use a period and extension, or you might confuse directories with filenames at some later date. Files and subdirectories in one directory can have the same names as files and subdirectories in other directories.

The form of the command depends on whether you are working in the directory below which you want to make a directory or subdirectory. For example, if you wanted to create the directories shown in the figure "Making Directories," you would type:

**Making Directories**

This tree shows the root directory, a LETTERS, MEMOS, and REPORTS directory, and two subdirectories, NEW and OLD.

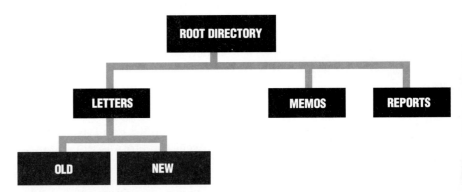

- **MD\LETTERS** and press [Enter←]
- **MD\MEMOS** and press [Enter←]
- **MD\REPORTS** and press [Enter←]

To make the two subdirectories off the LETTERS directory, you would type:

- **MD\LETTERS\NEW** and press [Enter←]
- **MD\LETTERS\OLD** and press [Enter←]

If you had first changed directories so that LETTERS was the default directory, you could make the two subdirectories by typing:

- **MD NEW** and pressing [Enter←]
- **MD OLD** and pressing [Enter←]

→ K E Y / S t r o k e s

### Making Directories

- To create a directory below the root directory regardless of the directory you are in, type **MD\** <*directory name*>.
- To create a directory below the root directory of another drive, type **MD** <*drive:\directory name*>. For example, to create a directory named 1-2-3 on drive C when drive B is the default drive, type **MD C:\1-2-3** and press [Enter←].
- To create a subdirectory in the current directory, type **MD** <*directory name*>. For example, to create a subdirectory named BUDGETS below the 1-2-3 directory when 1-2-3 is the current default directory, type **MD BUDGETS** and press [Enter←].

### Removing Directories

To remove a directory, you use the internal command RMDIR <*directory name*> (or RD <*directory name*>). For example, to delete a directory named LETTERS, you would type **RD LETTERS** and press [Enter←]. To delete a subdirectory named NEW below a directory named LETTERS, you would type **RD LETTERS\NEW** and press [Enter←]. The directory you want to remove must not contain any files or subdirectories, and it cannot be the current default directory.